PAST LIVES

PAST LIVES

Everyday people's remarkable experiences

RUTH HELEN CAMDEN

inspired LIVING

ALLEN&UNWIN

First published in Australia in 2009

Allen & Unwin
83 Alexander Street
Crows Nest NSW 2065
Australia
Phone: (61 2) 8425 0100
Fax: (61 2) 9906 2218
Email: info@allenandunwin.com
Web: www.allenandunwin.com

Cataloguing-in-Publication data for this title is held in the National Library of Australia

ISBN 978 1 74175 701 9

Typeset in 11/13 pt Adobe Garamond Pro by Midland Typesetters, Australia
Printed by McPherson's Printing Group

10 9 8 7 6 5 4 3 2 1

CONTENTS

ACKNOWLEDGEMENTS

Firstly, an enormous thank you to all the people whose past lives and personal stories have contributed to this book.

Thank you to Maggie Hamilton for her coaching and encouragement in getting this book to happen in the first place.

Thanks also to editor Desney Shoemark for the clarity and fresh point of view she brought me, just when I needed it.

Also thank you to those who read the manuscript as a work in progress, and whose welcome input helped bring it into shape.

And, most importantly, thank you to Samuel Sagan, my teacher, who ushered me through the gates of perception into inner worlds where nothing is quite what it first seems and mysteries and surprises are everywhere.

INTRODUCTION

You don't change by solving your problems,
you solve your problems by changing.
Dr Samuel Sagan

In many cultures the existence of past lives is accepted as part of the natural order of the world. Human beings are regarded as essentially spiritual beings who are caught in the cycle of death and rebirth. Some traditions hold that there is potential for growth and change in that process of living and dying many times. Others say the human race is caught in an endlessly repeating loop.

In this book I do not enter into any discussion on theories of reincarnation nor, in fact, will I attempt to prove the existence of past lives. Instead I relate the experiences of people from a range of backgrounds and belief systems who have undergone past-life regression and found that their experiences enabled them to make positive changes in their present life. Seeing the past causes of their present issues, whether in early childhood or in some long-forgotten past life, has brought profound personal realisations and inner healings.

Not all past life therapy is the same, or works according to the same principles. The technique I use is called ISIS, a set of techniques developed by the Clairvision® School. ISIS is part of a group of techniques that make up the Clairvision Inner Space Techniques or IST. It is practised with a client and a facilitator (called a 'connector'). ISIS is an acronym for Inner Space Interactive Sourcing.

The concept of *inner space* is one of the foundations of ISIS. During sessions clients enter an internalised state of consciousness which allows them to bring normally hidden aspects of the subconscious into their conscious awareness.

Despite its depth, entering the inner space is not difficult. With the guidance of a qualified practitioner, most people reach the inner space in a few straightforward steps. They typically recognise the space by its dark blue or purple light and its feeling of peaceful expansiveness.

During an ISIS session, the client lies comfortably with closed eyes, while the connector sits close by. Connector and client enter the inner space and the session unfolds. Through dialogue and an *interaction* of subtle energies between the client, the connector and the space, emotions and habitual patterns of thinking and behaviour in the client are highlighted and explored. The connector asks questions, not to ascertain names, dates or places, but to help the client enter the experience more deeply.

Whether the issue in question is a repeating cycle of emotional reactions, a health problem or a personality trait, the direction is the same: to go back to its origin. The emphasis in ISIS is on finding when and how things began—going to their *source*. Working at this level, people experience profound releases and realisations that go beyond resolution of the original issue. They come in touch with parts of themselves, which are limitless, from where they can access profound vision and spiritual presence.

While it is possible to live with emotionally charged but buried memories for years or even lifetimes without being aware of them, these memories can be surprisingly close to the surface. When entering into the deep inner work of emotional healing, such as happens in ISIS, there is something beautiful about releasing these latent emotions. Freeing buried memories leads to finding precious parts of a person's being that have been aching to be acknowledged. When people allow those forgotten parts to come alive, they go much further than solving their initial problems, they liberate themselves from all sorts of semi-conscious attitudes and beliefs that had been limiting them.

With ISIS, seeing past lives—or seeing anything for that matter—is experiential. This is very different to receiving a past-life reading from someone else. As an ISIS client you see and feel for yourself. Here, 'seeing' does not necessarily imply seeing images. With inner vision, feeling, sensing and knowing are not only valid ways of 'seeing' but are, in fact, essential to the process. Seeing images without feeling anything tends to make for shallow experiences that do not bring change. This book tells many stories of people who saw and felt their past lives in some detail. These people did not have any rare or special ability for this. Their experiences usually emerged over a number of sessions and the more they learned to let go and flow with their experiences, the more they could see.

In the space of ISIS there are no imagination or visualisation techniques. You see and feel things as they are and as they happened. When you experience for yourself the circumstances that caused a negative pattern, it is not uncommon for that pattern simply to drop away, as if by itself. It has lost its influence.

Contrary to cliches about people discovering themselves to be the reincarnation of Cleopatra or Napoleon, experiences of famous past lives are practically non-existent in ISIS. As a rule you can expect to find your past selves were about as ordinary or extraordinary as you are in the present.

Regardless of who people see themselves as in the past, famous, infamous or ordinary, they are encouraged not to take these experiences too literally. The purpose of ISIS is healing and self-knowledge, not historical investigation. By keeping the emphasis on the elements of feeling and experience rather than names, dates and places, the process retains its integrity and the focus remains on personal healing. If people were to become too distracted by the stories unfolding in the sessions, they would risk missing the point of the process. Experience is what changes people, not intellectual knowledge alone. The purpose of seeing past lives is personal healing and self-knowledge.

There is a second reason for not getting too attached to the details of past-life stories. It is sometimes possible for people to 'catch' in the inner space past-life experiences that did not happen exactly as they saw them. Experiences can also be symbolic. When this happens, the lives people see are not random experiences, but bridges to aspects of themselves that have lain hidden. Whether deep wounds or exalted states of spiritual connection, some inner experiences are paradoxically easier to get in touch with through seeing past lives.

The names and details of the people whose stories are told in this book have been changed to protect their privacy and anonymity, while maintaining the spirit of their experience.

1 EXECUTION Jade

Jade's job as an assistant for a professional photographer had ended badly and she needed to understand why. She had been working there for over a year when her boss started to treat her differently. He wasn't offensive, but Jade knew he was sexually attracted to her. When he realised she didn't return his feelings Jade's boss had become demanding and critical of her work, behaving unreasonably at times. Remaining cordial hadn't helped, and withdrawing seemed to antagonise him. She dreaded going to work and in the end Jade saw no choice but to resign. She now worked alone, doing tedious but safe data entry.

Jade longed for a career with creativity. Although she had a degree in marketing and media studies and dreamed of working in that field, she repeatedly found herself in low-grade clerical jobs. Something would always go wrong with her co-workers and this would block any chance she had of advancement. Besides, now she was just too tired for real creativity to flow.

Young, beautiful and intelligent, Jade looked capable of achieving whatever she wanted with her life. Instead she was struggling. For the last nine years she had been plagued with fatigue and depression. Around the time her health troubles started her boyfriend had dumped her, sending her spiralling into depression and bulimia. Feeling fat, unlovable and out of control, Jade had started the rounds of health practitioners, looking for a way to regain her health and wellbeing. Finally her doctor referred her to an IST practitioner for ISIS.

Jade's issue with relationships, however, concerned her even more. For as long as she could remember, things would be going along normally, then suddenly someone would turn on her and the relationship would sour. This had happened with friends, work colleagues and bosses. Each time she fell out with a friend or co-worker she became overwhelmed with fatigue again. Jade couldn't see how or why, but she sensed she must be causing these negative dynamics. She was trying so hard to turn things around and desperately needed a different perspective on life.

Like many clients, Jade had seen numerous practitioners. She was hoping this visit would not turn out to be yet another waste of time.

Jade was asked to lie down and relax and the session began. With her eyes closed she was guided into the inner space, an inner state of awareness where normally hidden parts of the subconscious become perceptible. After a few minutes Jade felt a sense of sadness and gradually a stream of impressions and emotions began to flow.

Jade had the feeling of being somewhere cold and grey. It felt to her like a cave or cellar, with damp rock walls. She saw a young mother and her two children, a girl and a boy, all terrified. Standing in front of them was a dirty, angry-looking man. The man seemed to be enjoying frightening the children by threatening them with all the things he might do to them. He told the mother she had better cooperate or he would kill the little boy in front of her. Prodding the mother with his gun, he sneered. The children screamed but the man just laughed. Desperate to keep her children safe, the mother held them tightly against her side.

Immersed in the experience, Jade was reliving the young mother's fear and feeling her powerful love for her son and daughter. What terrified the woman most was the prospect of this brute harming her precious children.

Then Jade felt the woman's fear deepen into a terrible sadness as the images of the children and the stone wall softly faded and everything became still. Now Jade had tears streaming down her cheeks. Although she couldn't yet see what had happened, she knew the danger had passed.

The woman—and simultaneously, Jade—felt herself surrounded by a great stillness where there was no need to move or speak. Jade welcomed the stillness and allowed it to soothe her sorrow.

As soon as Jade looked for the children she was back in the cave. This time she was looking down at the scene. The two traumatised children were alone in the darkness. At their feet was her dead body. A small trickle of blood ran from beneath her chest, forming a darkish pool on the floor. The man was gone.

Although she was no longer alive, the woman whom Jade felt as her past self could see everything as clearly as ever. She saw her children sobbing as the reality of what had happened sank in. Their mother was dead. Their father was away and the dangerous men were still in the house. What were they going to do?

Despite the horror of what had just happened, the young mother was surprised to learn that dying was not difficult. Nothing could hurt her now. Death had made her safe. What disturbed her was that she was powerless to help her beautiful children. She tried to whisper to them that she loved them, and to gather them in her arms like she used to, but it had no effect. Transfixed by shock, the children could only stare at their mother's body. Had they been less distraught they would have realised her presence was still right there with them.

For the woman, abandoning her beloved children was deeply painful. Leaving them unprotected and in danger went against everything in her. She ached with love for them. If only she could hold them once more, make the world safe for them again. But it was impossible.

Jade could feel the young mother's loss as strongly as if it were happening to her now. The overwhelming sadness came from deep within her. She had carried it with her through time. Although Jade had never been aware of this past life before now, the pain was all too familiar. That woman's sense of loss was the same as Jade had felt at twenty-one when her first boyfriend had left her. In fact, it was the same sorrow she had felt at the end of every relationship since then.

The grief kept pouring out of Jade in a jumble of tear-filled memories. She had carried the weight of this sadness for too long. Letting it go was an immense relief. As she cried, the pain in Jade's heart slowly subsided and was replaced by a deep peace.

Jade became silent as the atmosphere in the room became soft and vibrant. The silence had its own magic, like a rainbow after the rain. It brought the healing Jade was looking for. She felt her body relax like never before. By facing the difficult emotions she had buried for so long she was finally able to let them go. It felt so good.

Afterwards, Jade sat up, reflective. She was amazed at how clear her experience had been. The young mother's love for her children, her desire to protect them and her fear of the man had been so real. It was amazing to experience time dissolve like that. As she spoke, Jade's eyes were filled with joy. She felt amazing. She remembered feeling like this sometimes when she was a small child in bed at night, cocooned by the velvety darkness. Her grandmother used to tell her it was a time when angels could visit. She had forgotten how good it felt until now.

The terror Jade had felt in the cave was familiar too. She thought of times in her childhood when she had gone to stay with friends overnight. The minute a friend's father arrived home from work, she would panic and beg to be taken home. No matter what anyone said, young Jade couldn't relax until she was safe at home again. The irrational fear Jade had felt when faced with a strange man was the same awful sense of dread she had experienced as that woman in the cave when confronted with the man's death threats.

Thinking back over her experience in the cave, Jade realised that the fear and sorrow of the young mother were still a part of her now. They shaped her emotions and reactions in all sorts of circumstances. This was a powerful realisation for Jade.

A lot had happened for Jade in one session and she was given time to sit and let it sink in. Before she left she was asked to keep some ongoing awareness of the things that had been uncovered. As she went about her daily life, it was suggested Jade take notice if there were times when she felt the past-life woman's fear and sadness. Jade should see which situations highlighted or triggered her emotions. This, it was explained, would make it easier for her to continue with the same experience in the next session.

It wasn't yet clear what the relevance could be between Jade's experiences in this session and the difficulties she had been experiencing with co-workers. She wanted to know and promised to be aware of the woman she had once been until the next meeting.

2
A COURAGEOUS DECISION
Jade

A week later Jade practically bounded into the room, eager to start. It had been a good week. She had been feeling reasonably healthy and more positive than in a long time, even being inspired to meditate a few times.

During the week Jade had been in some situations where she felt just like the woman she had seen in the last session. In particular, she noticed that she was easily unsettled by a certain man at her workplace. She had always thought him shifty and didn't like being around him. This week, in the light of what she had seen about her past, Jade had realised this unease she felt around her co-worker was coming straight from the trauma she had experienced as that desperate mother in the cave. It was the same mechanism that had made her afraid as a child. Jade had carried the fear across lifetimes and it was still a part of her now.

Jade was asked to lie down and close her eyes for the session. After a few minutes sinking into the inner space, Jade's experience began with something quite different to the cave scene. This time there were impressions of a little girl standing at the front gate of a house and Jade had the sense she was seeing herself in yet another life. The girl was wearing a red coat that came down past her knees, and a matching hat. In her right hand she held a small suitcase.

When asked how it felt to be that little girl, Jade found herself immediately enveloped in a feeling of peace. At the same time she noticed a woman dressed in black who was sobbing. Jade knew this was the girl's mother. She had lost her daughter and she would never see her again.

The dead child felt serene. She was happy to move on from her earthly life. The child only wished she knew how to reassure her mother there was nothing to be sad about. After a long illness, death had been sweet. She had simply drifted into a beautiful, gentle place, leaving all the sickness and distress behind. The coat and suitcase, Jade realised, were symbols of the little girl's departure.

As Jade basked in the sense of peace that surrounded the child, she noticed how similar this feeling was to her experience of the death of the woman in the cave. In an instant she was back there once more. Again she was the terrified mother backed against the wall. This time new impressions came pouring in. It was the Second World War, Jade now saw, and the man was in the uniform of a Nazi soldier. She felt her past self standing with her clinging children, facing the armed man. The place was not a cave, but the cellar of the family home.

Over the next few sessions more details emerged and slowly the chain of events was pieced together. Each session ended with Jade being surrounded in a soft peace, and when she cried that peace filled her heart. The woman had been at home when three soldiers banged at the door demanding to know where her husband was. She told them she didn't know, but the soldiers forced their way in. Two of them started to search the house room by room, while the third soldier ordered the family downstairs to the cellar. Lining them against the wall at gunpoint, he ordered the young woman to tell him where her husband was. When did she expect him to return? She protested that she had no idea, but he didn't believe her. Again and again he asked her, becoming increasingly aggressive and threatening to shoot her unless she told him what he wanted to know.

Although the woman didn't know where her husband was, she knew what he was doing. The couple were part of an underground railroad helping Jewish people escape from the Nazis. They had begun by helping a few Jewish friends who found themselves on the run for their lives and had soon found themselves organising a full-scale operation. She and her husband had pledged to each other to protect the refugees, even if it meant risking their own lives. They had been sheltering three families when her husband had received word that they were no longer secure. That night he was away, taking the fugitives to a safe haven.

Even though she was afraid for her children, the young mother was glad the families had escaped in time. Now here she was, facing death for her actions. She had always prayed it would not come to this. The soldier standing in front of her was convinced there was a secret hiding place somewhere in the house. He made ugly threats to the young mother, hoping to force a confession from her or perhaps draw her husband out of hiding.

Enraged that a defenceless woman was getting the better of him, the infuriated soldier shot her in the chest. Jade, experiencing everything just as her past self had, felt herself dying. She noticed how strange it was that she felt no pain. One moment she was facing the soldier's gun, and the next she was floating towards the ceiling as her body fell to the stone floor. She could see her stricken children and she was gripped with anxiety for them and her husband. It was more than she could bear to think about.

Jade was asked if the woman had been tempted to tell the soldier what he wanted to know. She answered with conviction. The woman hated the Nazis and what they stood for.

Even if it cost her her life, there was no way she was going to tell them a thing. The bare truth was, she didn't know where her husband was or when he'd be back.

As she spoke, Jade *was* the woman refusing to speak in the face of death. This was a side of Jade that hadn't surfaced so far: a woman sure of her principles and ready to defend them. It was inspiring. It was a glimpse of the Jade to come.

After the session Jade thought about the times in her life when she had been strong and determined like that woman of the past. She smiled as she recounted what an idealist she had been in her university days. Before her health failed, Jade had campaigned against child labour in undeveloped countries and supported human rights advocacy groups. In recent years, though, she had all but forgotten what it was like to have so much enthusiasm for something.

There was a noticeable difference in Jade during the weeks that followed. She seemed to be smiling more. She even looked younger. When told that she was shining, Jade agreed wholeheartedly. She had more vitality than in years. Friends were starting to ask what she was doing to look so good. Her emotional life was less turbulent too. These days when things went wrong, Jade tended to be annoyed or amused rather than weak or tearful, simply because she felt stronger inside.

Jade found it fascinating and slightly ironic that each week in her session she would see terrible things and feel painful emotions, and yet in the rest of her life she was feeling so good—better and better in fact. This was because Jade was discarding some of her heaviest emotional baggage. It was natural that she would feel lighter.

Jade wanted to understand more about how seeing an emotional trauma from a past life could help her feel better. How exactly did that work?

It was explained that traumatic events leave imprints—called 'samskaras'—in the subconscious. Even though an event may be buried and long-forgotten, the samskaric imprint remains. Whether people remember the event or not, the samskara it created has a lasting effect on their attitudes and behaviour. It locks them into an ongoing pattern of conditioning, for example, of defeat, hurt or conflict.

Before seeing this past life, Jade hadn't known about the samskara itself, even though she was aware of some of its effects: her childhood fears, for example, and her distrust of the man at work. Unaided, Jade had no way to see the imprint. Like a rock submerged in a river, it was creating ripples in her life while the cause remained hidden.

Jade's outlook was hopeful. Although nothing had changed in her outward circumstances, the quagmire of fatigue and emotions in which she had been caught was finally diminishing. She felt more energetic and positive than in years.

Despite this, Jade could see the old patterns were continuing to operate at work. She didn't like her job and felt misunderstood by her co-workers, but she still couldn't see exactly how she was creating the conflict. When told that it was not surprising that a problem that has developed over lifetimes should take more than a few weeks to set straight, Jade said this sounded reasonable. She was making all sorts of discoveries about herself and had decided to give some priority to this process of self-discovery for a while. A brighter future was promising to emerge. Jade was already looking forward to her next session.

3
SHATTERED DREAMS
Jade

Jade arrived for her next session announcing she had just applied for a new job. It was a position as a personal assistant in a large marketing firm, which promised to be both challenging and exciting. Although she would be employed in a junior role, Jade had high hopes it might lead to better things.

This time when the session began, Jade's lower belly started to ache as if she had been struck there very hard. It wasn't just the blow that made her feel sick, it was the sense it had come from someone she loved, although this didn't make any sense to Jade. As she stayed with the nausea, Jade's initial impressions grew clearer and soon she saw a distraught young woman sitting alone. The woman was clinging to her chair and sobbing.

Jade felt the woman's distress and knew she was seeing herself in another life. She felt her hands gripping the chair so tightly that her fingers were numb. She was sitting in a sparsely furnished room with a small table and two more chairs. In the corner stood an ancient piano.

Despite the sadness that welled up inside her, Jade couldn't help but laugh at the young woman's appearance. She was wearing a voluminous yellow dress and a ridiculously large hat decorated with red and yellow feathers that hung down over her face. Jade's laugh quickly faded when she felt why the woman was hiding behind the hat. She wanted so much to be gay and flamboyant like her clothes but inside she felt desolate. She had dragged herself onto the chair after being knocked to the floor by her husband.

Stunned by his cruel behaviour, the young wife asked herself what had gone wrong. She was despised by the man in whom she had placed her hopes and dreams. Although barely twenty, she felt old and defeated. As the woman's bitter tears fell Jade was also crying, shedding an old pain held deep inside. This was the first time Jade had seen anything about this past life, but the pain and sense of worthlessness were very real to her. It was a relief to allow it to surface at last.

Over the next few sessions the scene of the woman crying returned to Jade. Even before any image came she would begin to relive the woman's loneliness and self-loathing. The past-life woman was young and pretty but she felt drab and unloved. Her husband was older than her and he treated her like a child. She was often afraid of him.

When they married she had been scarcely more than a girl, her head filled with dreams of romance and babies. But the reality of married life turned out to be very different. Her husband wanted someone to bear his children and grace his arm on social occasions. A pretty young wife was a social asset. He had never expected his new spouse would be so needy and immature. Behind her poised grace she was not the self-assured woman he had expected, but an insecure girl.

For the young woman's part, she was dismayed to find her new husband so controlling. The charming man who had wooed her turned into a harsh and critical father figure. She had been duped by his distinguished looks and smooth manners. The young woman tried harder and harder to look her best and to be the wife her demanding husband seemed to want. Makeup and bright clothes didn't save her from feeling worthless and despised, however, and the more she tried to please her husband, the more irritating he seemed to find her.

From her present-day standpoint, Jade could empathise with the husband's frustration. His new wife was more in need of a nanny than a husband. At the same time she felt herself as the young woman, caught up in her emotional turmoil and unable to see further than her own problems.

As her marriage disintegrated the young woman's self-esteem plummeted. She turned into a shadow of the happy girl she had once been. Life with this man was a prison of criticism and contempt. She now loathed her young beauty. She hated her body and the life it had brought her, but she could see no way out.

To Jade the self-loathing was uncomfortably familiar. The unpleasant feeling that she didn't belong inside her own skin was exactly the way she had felt when she had been bulimic. She used to eat and eat, wanting to block out how bad she felt inside. When that didn't work she would throw up, trying to get rid of the ugly sensation in the pit of her stomach. Although she hadn't induced vomiting for some years Jade could recall exactly how it felt.

A few days after this session Jade called to say that the emotions of that young bride were so real that at times she almost wondered which life she was living. It was both disorienting and amusing. Jade asked if she was doing something wrong. Not at all, she was reassured. Besides being a normal part of the work on samskaras, a person's awareness of being in two lives simultaneously is a precious experience. It widens horizons and expands the sense of self-identity.

Jade arrived for the next session looking jubilant. The week had brought all sorts of realisations about herself. The common thread between the past and the present was self-worth or, rather, the lack of it. No matter what she did in her life, Jade always felt inadequate. Something was empty inside her. That young woman in the yellow dress had tried to fill her emptiness with dreams of a happy marriage. During Jade's bulimic years she had tried to fill it with food. The same emptiness had driven her to therapy.

At work, Jade had noticed she was feeling differently about the 'sleazy' work colleague whose manner had always seemed vaguely threatening to her. As she saw more about the underlying samskara that man had started to appear more awkward than sly, and her discomfort was turning to indifference.

Jade described how lately her shoulder had been giving her pain. Interestingly, it was more troublesome when she was in the inner space of ISIS—a classic sign the pain was related to an emotional blockage.

This time, once immersed in the inner space, Jade saw the young woman in the yellow dress early in the evening, getting ready to go out with her husband. She had just learned she was pregnant and was filled with a new sense of hope. She planned to tell her husband that evening and anticipated how pleased he would be. Her mood was light-hearted. Maybe a baby would make him love her and bring her happiness.

Her husband, however, was stern. Tonight they were going to a society ball and it was a serious event, he reminded her. A lot of important people would be there and she was expected to behave appropriately. She decided to delay telling him about the baby. Maybe once his social obligations were fulfilled he would be more relaxed. But things didn't go the way the young woman expected.

At the ball the husband went to speak with the other men, leaving his wife among the women. He kept looking in her direction and frowning. She wondered what she was doing wrong. Was she smiling too much? Not enough? She tried to look grown up but that didn't seem to work. Her gay mood evaporated as anxiety took over. Her husband came over and whispered in her ear that she looked ridiculous. None of the other women were dressed so flamboyantly, he said. She was making him into a laughing stock. She cursed herself for wearing this outfit to such a formal function. If only she could disappear into the walls. Her husband turned to the other women and began to joke with them about his wife's larger-than-life hat. She could have died of shame.

The rest of her evening was spent watching him dance with other women and charm them with his gallant manners. The joy she had felt at the new life growing inside her was gone. She felt small. Her belly started to hurt. She wanted to go home.

Once home her husband started to pressure her for sex. She wasn't feeling well and tried to dissuade him, telling him she might be pregnant. Instead of being delighted at the prospect of becoming a father, he accused her of making up excuses to avoid him. She stared at him in dismay. This was not going at all the way she had imagined. They started to argue. He grabbed her by the arm and pulled her towards him. When she protested he lost his temper and tore her dress. Pushing her away in disgust, he called her a foolish child with the intelligence of a sparrow. She was not even worth making love to. He punched her hard in the belly and she stumbled and fell, wrenching her shoulder as she hit the floor.

Without a backward glance her husband turned and walked away. The woman was stunned and sore. He had never hit her before. Everything was hurting: her shoulder, her belly and her heart. In shock, she struggled to pull herself together and get up onto the chair. Her husband was gone and she was alone with her pain. Devastated, she longed to run away, but there was nowhere for her to go. She wished she could hide and never have to look in a mirror again.

All her efforts to be the perfect wife had counted for nothing. She hated herself to the core. Even being alive was uncomfortable. She felt she didn't belong in her own life, her own body. Identifying with the young woman, Jade again recognised that sensation from her present life.

The husband stayed out all night. When he returned the next morning he behaved as if nothing had happened. But the young woman knew things would never be the same. After that night, each time the woman didn't meet her husband's high standards he would lose his temper and strike her. Sometimes he would tell her she was lucky to have him—a less generous man would never tolerate such a fool. She tried to keep the peace but it was so easy to anger him. For a while she kept hoping he might miraculously return to the gallant and charming gentleman who had courted her, but it never happened.

The young woman lost the baby. Her husband contemptuously blamed her for not taking proper care of herself. He told her no baby would want to stay in the womb of such a mother. She felt so beaten that at times she almost believed him.

The husband started spending more and more time away. Despite his callous behaviour the young woman was devastated each time he left. Her hopes for a baby and a happy family life faded. Now she was more alone than ever. She felt trapped in a life she hadn't chosen.

Although Jade had never been in an abusive relationship like this, she was astounded to see that many of her present emotions were exactly the same. That woman was still a big part of her. Jade's self-loathing made it impossible for her to get close to anyone. Her boyfriend was loving and patient and, although she did care for him, she realised that she had never really given herself fully in return. She resolved that from now on she would be as open to him as she knew how, even when it made her feel vulnerable.

In Jade's next session she was directed to see what had

become of the woman later in that life. Jade saw her past self many years later. She was sitting alone sewing, bent over by the weight of the past. She had lost everything: her youth, her beauty and her dreams. Her husband had gone to a distant country for business and she knew he would not be coming back. The loss of her dreams, the long years of abuse and self-hate had taken their toll. She had no close friends and her family lived far away. The woman lived alone with her bitter memories.

Although Jade's circumstances were nothing like that woman's, the woman's hopeless self-loathing had stayed with her. This time round it had manifested in her difficulties relating to others, the ongoing depression and fatigue, and even her eating disorder.

From time to time Jade reflected on the positive impact of experiencing these past events. Things were looking up. The shoulder pain which had appeared when she first saw that abusive past-life relationship had gone. More significantly, Jade's heart felt lighter. She had described it as a huge reservoir of heavy emotions and now, little by little, it was being emptied. Her boyfriend had noticed the changes and he loved the joyful side of Jade that was emerging. One evening he told her, 'Now you're the person I always knew you were.'

Besides the growing sense of love in her life, Jade was feeling different within herself. As the emotions that had fuelled the bulimia diminished in intensity, she was much more free about how and what she ate. It was the same when it came to choosing her clothes and how she spent her money. They were all things she used to feel strangely uneasy about, as if some disapproving figure was looking over her shoulder. Not any more. It was her life and she had the right to enjoy it. These were big changes for her.

Things were also going well on the professional front. Jade was now working for a marketing company with people who loved having her on their team. Her boss told her she was over-qualified for the job and recommended she apply for a senior position. Because Jade was more at peace with herself, she was relating to others in a harmonious way. The workplace troubles she had described in her first meeting now seemed ancient history.

Jade couldn't say exactly when the changes had happened, nor could she pinpoint one particular session that had brought about the shift, yet she felt different. Jade's boyfriend had described it perfectly: Jade was becoming her real self.

4
DEATH AT THE GALLOWS
David

David was a fit twenty-seven-year-old police rescue worker. In his free time he trained in martial arts and was proud to have recently earned his black belt in aikido. Not a man inclined to take things easy, David had been on several mountain climbing expeditions in the Himalayas and had ambitions to tackle Mount Everest. He spent his holidays taking groups of teenagers on rock climbing and white water rafting trips. At times his neck gave him a bit of trouble but it never stopped his active lifestyle.

Late one summer evening David's unit was called to a fire in a city apartment block. The building was old and unstable and the team's first priority was to get the occupants out fast. David was helping a family to safety when a section of roof collapsed. A heavy wooden beam bounced off another and hit him in the back of his neck. In the urgency of the moment David didn't realise he was injured, however once everyone was standing safely on the street the pain kicked in. It kept him awake most of the night and by morning it was excruciating.

Work was out of the question. The slightest movement of his head gave him shooting pains, and even sitting for more than a minute was unbearable. For someone who liked to exercise every day this was immensely frustrating. Spending days lying flat on his back was not David's idea of a good time.

David's doctor diagnosed a slipped disc and sent him to a physiotherapist. After seven long weeks of rest and daily physiotherapy, however, David's neck wasn't much better. He was bored and frustrated. There must be a faster way. Through his aikido training he had learned to feel subtle flows of 'chi', or life force, and even before the accident he had noticed a blocked energy right where his neck had been hurt. He wondered what sort of strange coincidence would cause the injury to happen right in that spot.

David was not a newcomer to working in the inner space. He had done several courses in the past and had practised the technique extensively with fellow students. He recognised it offered the ideal approach to look at his neck injury from a different perspective.

David moved stiffly as he sat down to begin the session. He frowned as he carefully positioned himself so that he did not have to turn his head.

For David the worst thing about his neck pain was the acute sense of hopelessness it brought. He guessed this was to be expected, considering he could hardly move without pain. He was surprised to hear otherwise. Reactions to pain are subjective. One person might become angry, another may worry and a third may try to escape the pain through alcohol or drugs. David was intrigued. He had never thought of questioning the way he felt. There might be more to this injury than he had imagined.

When David lay down and turned his awareness inwards, being horizontal didn't bring the relief it normally did. Instead his neck started to hurt even more. He could have sworn there was pressure against his throat, even though nothing was touching him there. The sensation intensified until the tightness felt like a noose around his neck. David had the sense he was someone about to be hanged and the experience started to flow.

David felt himself as a teenaged boy, perhaps thirteen, standing at the gallows. The boy was crying and shaking uncontrollably. In a few moments he would be swinging by a rope, along with his parents and older brother. Not only was the lad petrified, he had no idea what he had done wrong.

Over the next few sessions a story emerged. The boy lived with his parents and brother on a remote ranch where they worked hard to make a living from the arid brown hills. A conflict developed between the boy's father and some neighbouring landowners about the family's right to be on the land. One day the neighbours came to the property and confronted his father. Talking escalated to argument, voices were raised and ugly threats were made. The boy's father was a simple man. He was not used to fighting, but after this he began to sleep with his gun by his pillow and he carried it with him when he rode out on the ranch.

A few weeks later several officials in dark suits arrived at the house and arrested the whole family on the pretext of illegal occupation of the land. They were handcuffed and led behind the horses to town, two days' walk away. That night they stopped next to a river to sleep. The ground was cold and hard and there was nothing to eat. The boy had no idea what he had done wrong. Why were they being treated like criminals? Had his father really broken the law? His parents were no comfort. They seemed to be even more afraid than he was.

Around sunset on the second day they arrived at the town. Instead of receiving an explanation, the family was thrown into a lockup and left there. Someone brought them food and water but there was no word of any kind of a trial or hearing.

As he relived the ordeal David was struck by the passivity

of the boy's family. They let themselves be treated like cattle. They saw no way to fight the system so they simply gave up, waiting for their fate and leaving the boy to go through his own private hell.

A few days later the frightened family was brought to the gallows without any questioning or trial. An official read out the charges and declared the four were to be sentenced to death by hanging. At the sight of the four nooses hanging ready the boy was stricken with terror. Among the small crowd that had gathered to watch he recognised the faces of the men who had started all this trouble. Completely overwhelmed, the boy wavered between helplessness and sheer panic. Why did these people want him to die? He had done nothing against them.

The noose was put around his neck and a hush fell over the crowd. The boy felt the rope being drawn tight against his throat and heard the sounds of his older brother sobbing next to him. The wooden platform dropped from under his feet and he fell. There was an awful crunch as his neck broke.

David suddenly relaxed and the atmosphere in the therapy room changed. The panic was gone and a strange mixture of impressions took over. There was a sense of floating in space. The boy's neck hurt and he could hear a crowd cheering and someone crying, but it seemed to be happening far away. Strangely, he wasn't struggling or gasping for air although he was dizzy and his lungs wanted oxygen. There was no sensation anywhere below the neck. He could feel his body was starving for air, but it seemed not to belong to him any more. Too late for struggle, too late for hope. He felt himself drifting away from his body.

There was nothing peaceful about this letting go. The boy fell into a strange kind of limbo. His familiar body sensations were gone. His mind swam with distorted images of the last few terrible days. Finally, grateful to remember something familiar, the boy turned to the land he knew so well. Sometimes it had seemed almost a friend to him. The empty landscape had shared his thoughts on many a solitary ride across the ranch. He let himself drift, his consciousness spreading into the landscape, until eventually it too faded away and he was drifting in nothingness.

After seeing these strange limbo spaces David sat up and thought about his present life. The resignation he had felt as that young boy was too familiar. When things got too much he often felt like giving up and just waiting for fate to take over.

It was pointed out that David's life so far didn't indicate he was someone who gave up easily. Even when his neck had brought a halt to his active lifestyle, he still spent hours each day doing physiotherapy and relaxation exercises. Not much apathy there.

David agreed. Even so, he often felt victim to things beyond his control. The neck pain made him feel that way, and so did his job. At work his superiors told him what to do, where he would be stationed and when to take time off. Like the boy on the gallows, David felt he couldn't do a thing to change the system.

With a sigh David elaborated on the hopelessness he felt. Nothing he did for his injury seemed to help and it looked like he had lost a girlfriend too. Just before the injury he had started dating someone, but now when he called she was always busy. His love life had become one more thing to feel hopeless about.

In his following sessions David returned to the scene on the gallows. When the boy realised he was about to die for something he hadn't done and had no control over, he gave up all hope. As he drifted into death his last lucid thought was to wonder at the injustice of it all. Surely there could be no good in a world where things like this can happen?

David explored the boy's childhood. It had not been a joyful one. David saw endless days of work. The boy's mother was always complaining and his father seemed to favour his older brother. Laughter was not often heard in the home. The boy preferred to spend his time riding his horse in the hills. Interestingly, the more David felt the child's sadness, the less his neck hurt during the sessions. Sometimes he would have tears of grief rolling down his face and the neck pain would almost disappear. It seemed most of the pain was not coming from the neck, but the sad heart of a lonely boy.

David was asked to go to a time when his heart had been strong. Suddenly he was in a vast darkness, like outer space, moving very fast towards Earth. He was heading towards a new life. There was no sign of hopelessness. David felt an exhilarating sense of freedom. He was unstoppable. The fullness and joy was a million miles from David's recent despondent mood.

He landed in the womb of his mother in that lifetime on the ranch. At first he was loved and wanted. It was going to be a good life. But then an older sister, still a baby, became ill and died. The boy's mother was devastated and she closed down. Broken-hearted herself, she was unable to give anything to her unborn child. The boy was born already starving for love. Over time his joy faded and his heart grew cold and small.

As David felt his past self longing for love, something started to awaken in his heart. The inner space turned bright and fiery. It surrounded David with compassion and he cried tears of relief. Time seemed to stand still. The fiery quality grew stronger and David had the sense of something emerging in his heart, like a flaming orange sun. It offered the joy and fullness he wanted so much but his chest still felt too small to let it shine.

Over David's next few sessions the hopelessness and grief came up again. Each time he was able to let a little more of the pain out of his heart. At the end of each session the same fiery sun-heart quality would fill the space, ever more intensely. David was reconnecting with an essential part of himself that had been lost for so long—his hope.

Over the weeks David's attitude of resignation decreased markedly. He was moving and walking with a spring in his step and a grin on his face. He was still taking painkillers for his injury, but the pain was slowly diminishing. However, David was no longer resigned to living with circumstances the way they were, and he had started to make plans to change other things in his life. He began to talk about new career options that offered more scope for his sharp intellect. One day he announced that he had decided to retrain as a computer programmer. Strikingly, as the hopelessness lessened, so did the neck pain.

Soon David was too busy studying to continue his sessions. Besides, he had met someone new at his programming course and was looking forward to spending more time with her.

5
SAMSKARAS

A boy is ten years old. His dog has just died and no one seems to understand how he feels. Terribly alone, he cries over his loss and has some childhood realisations about life and death, love and loss. What might be the lasting effects of this event?

Maybe he longs for another dog. He insists he won't be happy until his parents find him one—it must be exactly the same. He pesters them until they agree.

Or he has the opposite reaction. Losing his four-legged friend was just too painful and he declares he *never* wants another dog. In his mourning, ten-year-old heart the boy decides the only way to prevent another loss like that is not to care that deeply about anything again.

Either way, the death of the beloved pet will have a lasting effect. The imprint it leaves is called a samskara—a stamp or scar in a person's psychological makeup. The samskara becomes part of the person, one of the many factors that shape his or her personality.

'Samskara' is a highly useful term from Sanskrit, the ancient literary language of India. A samskara is a psychological imprint created by a traumatic or, more accurately, an intense event. What creates a samskara is emotional intensity.

The word 'samskara' doesn't have a satisfactory equivalent in the English language. 'Emotional blockage' doesn't quite do it. To properly describe the mechanism a more precise term is needed. Choosing the right word is not just a question of translation. Along with any word comes a concept. Like 'karma', 'deja vu' or any number of foreign words adopted into the English language, the word 'samskara' allows English-speakers to talk about an idea that wouldn't otherwise exist in their culture.

Reflect again, then, on the boy's loss of his dog when he was ten. Later in life when his own children start asking for a dog, how will he respond? The death of his childhood pet may not be the first thing he thinks of, but the samskara it left behind still colours his attitude. Dogs create work and cost money, he objects. The children will become attached. In the end pets always die and make everyone sad. He refuses, saying he won't have dog hair all through the house. If the children want a pet they can have a goldfish.

Imagine how much greater the samskara would be if it was his mother he had lost at age ten. The impact would be massive. Later in life, the sense of abandonment created by that early loss might draw him to friendships with mother figures. Or the samskara may do the opposite—create mistrust with women and shake his sense of belonging in the world. Either way, the insidious influence of the samskara would show in his life.

Jade saw the origins of a samskara when she was the woman in the cellar unable to protect her children. She saw how another samskara was created during her life as the woman abused by her husband. At first the relevance of those past-life experiences to her present issues was not obvious. It took a number of sessions before her pattern of closing off from people became clear to her and things could begin to change.

Whatever the trauma, the essential mechanism is the same. The event creates an imprint (samskara), which conditions a person's attitudes and behaviour.

To be more precise, the samskara is created not by the event itself but the way a person reacts to it. Because human beings are not identical, the same incident affects people in varying ways. One individual might cry, another will shout, while a third may be unaffected. Young children are particularly impressionable and can be deeply damaged by relatively minor traumas, such as being left alone to cry in a scary place.

Once imprinted, a samskara continues to shape a person's emotions and behaviour indefinitely. This happens whether they remember the original event or not. Depending on the intensity of emotion, the effects of a samskara can be enormous and far-reaching.

In Jade's case, her unease around her 'sleazy' work colleague seemed minor. It wasn't affecting her work and she had never thought to question it. It was the same with her childhood fears, which she had all but forgotten. However, as soon as Jade saw the past-life samskara it became clear her emotional reactions represented something much larger. They signalled a deep-seated pattern of mistrust and closing off that was blocking Jade in her life. In order to shift the negative pattern, Jade first needed to find where it was coming from. She needed to see the reason for the samskara.

After Jade had done some sessions on this samskara she saw her co-worker with new eyes. What she had once labelled slyness she now recognised as insecurity. In fact Jade wondered how someone so innocuous could have appeared so threatening to her.

For David, his samskara of being hanged as an innocent child was latent most of the time. However, when he was caught in situations beyond his control the samskara would be triggered and the boy's hopelessness would surface.

How can reliving a trauma bring healing?

For some people the thought of going back into all the painful, frightening or confronting emotions seems crazy. Aren't those things best kept buried safely in the past? On the contrary, the traumas may be buried but far from safely. Their effects are very much alive in the present. Even when samskaras are well hidden their signs appear throughout a person's life.

It is not always easy to let old emotions resurface; however, when at last they are released, the sense of relief is enormous. Some people compare the feeling to being let out of a cage, or the sun coming out after the rain. In the long run, feeling the pain of a buried samskara is far less damaging than leaving it there.

Samskaras create an emotional quagmire that clouds clarity and disrupts free will. Most people are not able to choose whether to be sad, happy, angry or enthused. They live in the ever-changing colours of their own moods and attitudes. Pushing the reactions and emotions away does nothing to resolve them, it only buries them deeper. As long as the samskaric imprints exist, the emotional atmosphere created by them is always present behind the scenes.

People's likes and dislikes, attitudes and personality traits, and even their health problems, can have their roots in samskaras. With the resolution of each major samskara people come closer to living as the free human beings they are meant to be.

6
A COLD START TO LIFE
Sally

Sally was a middle-management executive in a financial investment company. She had worked hard and at forty-three had the lifestyle to prove it. She enjoyed professional respect from her colleagues and worked in a prestigious office with her own team. Her home was spacious and comfortable, she drove a luxury car and when she travelled she stayed in the best hotels. Sally's private life, on the other hand, was not going so well.

Since the end of her last relationship three years earlier, Sally had developed a number of phobias. A few months after the breakup, she became anxious and panicky when in enclosed or crowded places. Elevators and trains felt so oppressive that getting to work each day had turned into a nightmare. When her fears didn't pass, Sally had hypnotherapy and was also given a personalised mix of flower essences. She was relieved to see the claustrophobia and fear of crowds disappearing in a matter of weeks.

Not long after this Sally found herself being terrified by the sight of sharp knives, and this time the fear was more intense. Sally knew it was irrational but she couldn't help it. She tried to avoid the problem by carefully packing away her kitchen knives in a high cupboard and buying only groceries that didn't require cutting. This was no solution and Sally worried that if she got rid of the knife phobia like she had the claustrophobia, she might create something even worse. She needed a different approach without having to spend years in therapy. Could she have somehow triggered a buried trauma involving knives? Past-life therapy looked interesting and Sally decided to give it a try.

With her elegant blonde hair and expensive business suit Sally looked composed, not like a person riddled with fear. When she sipped her glass of water she didn't even leave lipstick on the rim. Sally was used to being in control of things and she found it unnerving to be thrown off balance at the mere sight of a knife in a drawer.

The phobias had started after a relationship breakup. When asked about her love life Sally pulled a face. All three of her long-term relationships had ended in heartache, the last one particularly badly. Since then Sally had hardly dared look at a man, instead throwing herself into her career where she knew how to make things work. The business world might have its let-downs but to Sally they were nothing compared with the troubles she had encountered in her love life.

Sally was a capable woman who was used to being in control. Now, to get the most from her sessions, she was going to have to learn a new approach. She was asked to let go of any ideas or expectations and to be open to whatever might come up in the session. Working at it in her usual style would not help here. This was the time to be receptive to whatever would emerge.

At the start of the session, Sally was guided into the inner space where the internalised state of awareness would allow her to see things that were normally hidden. After some time Sally began to feel cold and soon she was chilled to the core, as if she was inhaling frost into her lungs. She shivered, despite the warm day. Sally was directed back towards the time when the cold had started. The chill grew stronger and soon she had the feeling of being herself as a baby. She was lying on her back, naked and alone. Around her were the plain white walls of a hospital ward.

Sally felt strange in her baby body. It was small and soft. Her arms and legs didn't quite respond the way she wanted them to. Her mind felt different. It was not busy with thoughts but filled with a more peripheral awareness, receiving a myriad of sensations and impressions. In the background was the awful feeling that something was missing.

Baby Sally wanted so badly to be touched, to be held in someone's warm arms. Her little body was uncovered and there was an uncomfortably cold draft blowing over her bare skin. Inside her mother she had always been warm. Now everything was cold, so cold.

Sally had been born prematurely and had spent the first four weeks of her life in a hospital humidicrib. After the all-encompassing warmth of the womb, the antenatal ward of a public hospital was a cold and lonely start to life. The nurses seldom touched her or talked to her. Not one of them treated her like a real human being with her own needs and emotions.

Sally was shivering in the session and was covered with a warm blanket but she kept shivering. Baby Sally longed for her mother. Why didn't she come? Maybe she didn't want her. Why was she in this cold glass box? There was no human warmth anywhere, just a frigid cold that seemed to go on forever.

Sally was guided further back in time, to her mother's womb. She quickly relaxed and a contented smile came to her face. Inside the womb it was wonderfully protected. Her mother's presence surrounded her with love. This was where she belonged, merged in her mother's body warmth, safe and protected from the world, Sally was in no hurry to leave.

During the pregnancy Sally's mother was often sick and

had to lie quietly in bed. Once she spent a week in hospital. As an unborn foetus Sally didn't understand these things intellectually, but she could feel her mother was unwell and knew instinctively it was because of her. Her mother couldn't wait for the pregnancy to be over and Sally felt weighed down by the responsibility. Maybe she didn't belong here after all. She yearned to go home.

Feeling this, adult Sally paused. The sense of longing for home was so strong. But where was 'home'? Sally was asked to go further into that feeling of home. That was easy. Following the yearning, Sally was drawn back beyond the womb to a luminous dark space. The cold was left behind and a soft gold poured into her through the darkness. The beautiful light felt so warm and loving, Sally could hardly believe it. It took over the inner space, turning everything bright gold. Sally was fascinated. She embraced the light, letting it spread into her heart and feeling its liquid warmth thaw out the coldness.

After the session Sally sat up with a child-like smile on her face. That was nothing like she had expected. No knives, no phobia, no past life. But that gold . . . She had never seen anything like it. What was it about? What did it mean? How could she get more?

One of the best things about being a connector is when things like this happen. A session starts with looking for the source of a problem and leads to the discovery of a treasure.

The gold had brought a sense of healing to Sally, and her problem had been illuminated. It was clear that with a few more sessions like this, Sally's fear would end up fading by itself. But Sally was still curious about the knife phobia.

It was explained that fear is often a false problem. While the fear itself is real enough, trying to heal or get rid of it by looking for a trauma that caused it is not always fruitful. In Sally's case it appeared clear that the fear was due to an inner disconnection from herself. If that could be addressed the fear would go, like ice under the sun.

When Sally arrived for her next appointment she was smiling. What a week it had been. All day at work she kept remembering the liquid gold and it made her feel like smiling. Worrying about knives suddenly seemed absurd, yet Sally knew she was not over the phobia. The previous day she had felt confident enough to reach for a small sharp vegetable knife from her high storage cupboard, but at the last moment she just couldn't do it. Irrational or not, the knife fear was still a problem.

Sally talked for a while about the gold. The feeling it evoked reminded her of when she was a young teenager. She had grown up in a small seaside town and loved the magic hour of dawn on the beach. She used to sit on the sand dunes and look out to the horizon while the colours changed over the water. Sometimes she would write poetry. Relationships were not an issue in those days, she had her sunrises and poems. Her sense of inner wellbeing was strong then.

The session started by recalling the feeling of the gold. Soon Sally saw a crop of ripe wheat and felt herself as a young girl, perhaps fifteen years old. It was a warm sunny day and the girl was lying on her back in the middle of the wheat field. No one could see her, only the insects and the birds. In the distance were the sounds of farm workers calling to each other as they worked. She felt carefree and surrounded by love.

The girl, who was Sally in a former life, lived with her parents in a small farming community where all the families helped each other tending the crops, harvesting and going to market. The girl knew she was different from other people. Although she would soon be a woman, she had a strange chubby body and a round child-like face with eyes that squinted in a perpetual smile. She didn't go to school or work on the farms. She knew she wasn't clever like other people.

For her there were no responsibilities, just days spent playing in nature, lost in her own world. She knew her mother and father loved her. To them she was a joyful child who would never grow up. Her innocent nature was a gift from heaven.

The workers in the fields would wave to the girl as she wandered past. On summer afternoons she loved to lie in the ripening wheat, watching the clouds change shape as they drifted across the sky. She could lose herself for hours studying the way a caterpillar spins its cocoon. Life was safe, full of love and blissfully happy. The young girl who was Sally's past self knew other people didn't have this bliss. It was a shame they would never understand her world. She knew she was blessed.

In the following session Sally saw herself in the same life some years later. This time the girl was married to a gentle farm worker who loved and protected her. It didn't matter to him that she wasn't intelligent. To the man his wife was like a kind of magical nature spirit. He didn't expect her to be like everyone else. He just loved to be near her smile and feel her bliss.

She loved him too in her innocent way, however her greatest happiness came from being with nature. She would listen to the songs of birds and the wind in the trees as they whispered their wordless secrets. There were not many people who could hear them like she did, so the fields and forests poured their wisdom into her. To the girl it was a world of simple harmony and everything in it was part of the dance of nature.

After this Sally had several more sessions, visiting both the cold hospital crib and the life of the girl again. Each session started with the coldness and ended in the feeling of being deeply loved and nourished through nature.

These experiences touched Sally deeply, but she struggled to integrate them into her present situation. Living in the fields and writing poetry on the beach were not the answer to her present dilemma. Sally wanted to find peace and wellbeing *inside* herself. She joined a meditation class and began getting up early each morning to meditate. Quickly Sally noticed that starting the day like this made her feel remarkably good. A neglected aspect of herself was being nourished again. She felt more centred than she had in years. There was also a growing sense of being in the right place: a subtle knowing of her place in the creation.

In Sally's sessions, not once did traumas involving knives or enclosed spaces come up and yet her fears were steadily diminishing. She was happier and looked ten years younger. One day she retrieved her kitchen knives from their hiding place and knew it was over. No more phobias. Once she had found a source of wellbeing within herself, her anxiety had simply ceased to exist.

Sally reflected on her journey since her first session. The phobias had not been the 'real' problem, but a signal to dig deeper. Although a subtle person with a natural affinity for introspection, Sally had not realised how distanced she had become from her own inner life until rediscovering it in past-life therapy.

Besides these benefits, there was another result that Sally had not expected. She was becoming far less afraid of being hurt by others. It was time she met an interesting man, she decided.

In the end Sally's knife fear had nothing to do with knives at all, but with a general lack of inner harmony. Once this started to change, Sally's phobias vanished and she found a new freedom in her life.

7
DEATH ON THE WIRES
Teena

Teena had been thrown into a huge dilemma. A talented graphic artist for a cinema animation studio, she had just been offered a big promotion. The new job was Teena's dream, giving her the chance to work with the best. The hitch was that the position was in a city several hours flight away and Teena did not want to relocate.

She had just moved in with Kurt, her partner of three years. She loved him and hoped they would have a long future together. Kurt, a civil engineer, however, had recently signed a contract for a bridge-building project that was scheduled to take the next two years. Teena was faced with an impossible choice: to refuse a once-in-a-lifetime job or enter into a long-distance relationship. Who could tell if she and Kurt would still be as close in two years? She was caught between the love for her partner and her creative work. With all her heart Teena wished she didn't have to choose. She felt confused and sad.

In one of her ISIS sessions Teena saw herself sitting on the sawdust floor of an empty circus tent, crying as she cradled her dead lover in her arms. He had fallen while they were rehearsing for their circus act.

As Teena went deeper into the experience, she saw that it was late in the evening. The two performers had been on the trapeze high up among the ropes of the Big Top, practising a daring new move. But the man had missed his grip at the crucial moment and, horrified, Teena's past self watched as her partner's body plummeted into a pile of equipment. He was already dying when she reached him. He was unable to speak but his eyes met hers.

Everything became still. Even in her distress the young woman felt strangely peaceful. She held eye contact with her lover as the life left his body. The precious last moments seemed to last forever. Then he was gone. She stayed with him, rocking him in her arms and crying. It was the longest, darkest night of her life, yet she didn't want it to end.

Teena, feeling everything her past self had experienced, was also crying. Her left arm was hurting, just as the young trapeze artist's arm had ached with the weight of her lover's body as she held him.

At dawn the circus troupe found the young woman sitting with her dead lover. Although she assured them she was unhurt, inside she was broken. Everything felt strange and far away. Sometime after her friends carried her lover away—she didn't know how long—she got to her feet and slowly walked outside. She neither hesitated nor looked back. In that moment she turned away from her life in the circus, but she would never leave behind the impact of that terrible night.

Teena felt the young trapeze artist's shock. She had lost everything that mattered to her. The years with her beloved partner had been short but filled with adventure. From the first moment it was as if they had known each other forever. When they were travelling the country with the circus, the couple amazed the crowds with their skill and breathtaking acts. Their love for each other made them feel invincible. It shone through their performance and made them the most popular act of the circus. She was his darling. He was the centre of her world. Inspired by love, the young woman's creativity was never ending. She designed costumes, wrote music, choreographed dance routines for their act, and invented many new moves on the trapeze to entertain their audience.

Now, everything had changed. Circus life had led to tragedy and heartbreak. The performer resolved danger and risk would not be a part of her new life. She never wanted to go through anything like this again.

The trapeze artist took a train to get as far away as possible from everything she knew, but she didn't know how to leave behind the overwhelming grief and guilt. No one had blamed her for the accident but she felt responsible. They had been practising one more of her increasingly risky ideas.

The young performer's belief in herself was deeply shaken. Her darling was dead, killed by her own creativity. Ambition and success suddenly appeared to be a kind of greed that had destroyed the things she loved the most.

Teena's past self left behind not only her old life but also her artistic pursuits. Her life might as well be over. From now on she would just be waiting to die.

Next, Teena saw the young performer some years later, living in a small mountain village in a foreign country where no one knew about her circus career. Her passion for life was gone. Everywhere she looked she saw the same perpetual emptiness. The emptiness was inside her because she had turned away from a part of herself.

Life in the village was uncomplicated. No one spoke her language and there was nothing to trigger her memories. At first the woman made half-hearted attempts to write music, but this made her so sad she eventually put it all aside. She tried not to think about anything that reminded her of her old self.

It was easy for Teena to feel the link between the circus performer's life and her present situation. The trapeze artist had followed her passion and lost her love. Now Teena could face the same consequences for following her career. There didn't seem to be room in her life to have both art and love.

Teena explained this was not the first time she had faced this dilemma. At eighteen she had plunged into a graphic arts degree. Her boyfriend at the time had accused her of caring more for her studies than for him and had left her for another girl. Badly affected, Teena saw her marks take a dive. After that she put even more into her studies, and she never gave herself unreservedly to anyone again.

Teena had not understood it this clearly before, but she had always felt a conflict between having a love relationship and being free to follow her creative pursuits. She was plagued by the uneasy feeling that her art was self-indulgent and someone would be hurt because of it. Teena knew it was not rational, but this feeling still inhibited her creativity as well as prevented her from getting too close to anyone. The effect of feeling torn between love and creative pursuits was that she ended up having neither one fully.

It appeared that the trapeze artist had been so completely focused on her partner that she didn't know how to be happy without him. When Teena was asked if she could see similarities between her past self and herself now, she pulled a wry face and shook her head. Since that first boyfriend she had become so wary of being dependent on a partner that she gave out the impression she didn't need anyone. Whenever tensions arose between her and Kurt, she would become silent and withdrawn. Luckily Kurt was patient with Teena when she was in these moods. Teena would have liked to be more open with him but she honestly didn't know how.

Moreover, in each of her relationships Teena had been haunted by a small nagging thought: if a much loved partner was to leave or be killed she would be inconsolable, and she couldn't bear that. So she had carefully guarded her independence and took pride in never being jealous or possessive.

This, she realised, was not a sign of maturity but rather a sign that she had become too detached to experience jealousy.

Teena observed her moods during the week following this session. On a few evenings when she was alone she felt the trapeze artist's melancholy. Even through the sadness there was a sense of reconnection to a profound part of herself. It was a part of her that knew what pain was and, having felt the worst, was no longer afraid of it. In this sorrow Teena felt closer to her real self than she had ever felt in her independence.

When she arrived for her next session the sadness of her past self was close to the surface. After watching it in the background all week, it was easy for Teena to cry and simply let it go. This time the session ended with a beautiful experience. Teena was feeling the circus performer's grief and crying her tears. She was so merged with her past self that she could hardly say which one was more the real Teena. Then the space appeared to become vast like the night sky. Teena felt herself across time: two personalities with one soul and one future. She sensed the most dense and tangible stillness she had ever experienced. It made her feel spread across the inner space like a silent lake. Teena's breathing became almost imperceptible. Even the usual chatter of her inner thoughts was still.

Teena had let go so completely into the experience of her grieving past self that she was creating a bridge across time. A healing was taking place. It was time for Teena to reclaim the part of herself that had been shut away so long ago.

Lying there still and silent, Teena felt a kind of light emerging from deep within. It felt like an essential part of her soul coming back to life. Joy flooded the space and washed everything with light. She felt she was shedding several hundred years of emotional weight from her shoulders. When she sat up her eyes were shining.

After this Teena was so enthusiastic she did five more sessions in only two weeks. In each session she saw the same pattern: following her creativity and losing love because of it. Her current life had been no exception.

Teena was caught in a double bind. She distrusted her artistic side because she feared it distanced her from the people she loved, yet she couldn't live without creativity. She had often resented her loved ones because she perceived them as the ones who were making her choose. Teena now realised her dilemma was the result of her own distorted view. She had been playing out the same samskara for lifetimes. At last she felt herself becoming free of this negative pattern.

Several weeks after Teena's last session a message arrived from her. She had taken the interstate job and had managed to negotiate working hours that allowed her to visit Kurt every two weeks. He was organising to do the same so he could visit her every alternate week. Teena was finding a new level of trust and openness with Kurt and, moreover, this was bringing her a flood of ideas for stories and projects to create. Teena was finding that love, far from being a block to creativity, could be its inspiration.

8
FIGHTING FOR A LIVING
Eric

The softly spoken man on the phone inquired politely whether he needed to have a problem in order to look at his past lives, or was simple curiosity enough?

Eric had been wanting to do some past life therapy for a while but was a bit nervous about what he might see. He was sure that seeing his past would help him to understand himself better in the present, but he had a sneaking suspicion he might discover things about himself he wouldn't like. After wavering for months, he eventually decided that if there were demons inside he preferred to see them. Then, at the very least, he would know what they were.

As Eric lay quietly in the inner space of his first session it became immediately clear that there was a violent intensity in him. It lay completely hidden behind his gentlemanly manner. A slightly built man with a shy smile, it was hard to believe Eric worked in the cut-throat world of property speculation. He had been investing in property since his teens and by the time he was twenty had already made—and lost—his first million. Despite his hesitant manner it was obvious that when it came to business Eric was a predator. Yet, regardless of whether things were going well or badly, Eric worried. In business and in his private life he was plagued by anxiety.

There was nothing in Eric's life story to suggest he had ever been physically violent, yet it was easy to sense a force in him that could have made a small nation tremble. No doubt it was this he had been nervous about seeing. However, if he was to discover anything about himself, it would be through getting in touch with that violence.

Eric didn't have to go far to find it. As he immersed himself in the inner space, he started to feel as if his body was fit and well muscled. Impressions came to him of a hot place that was dusty and smelled of sweat. A bright light was shining on him and around him the semi-darkness was filled with a throng of noisy people. He was in a boxing ring, fighting.

The boxer was a thick-set man with a square jaw. He fought for a living but he would have also done it for sport. His angry temperament ensured he was one of the best fighters around. He was dangerous and his opponents knew it. Had he wanted, he could have killed any one of them.

In the beginning the boxer had not fought so aggressively; he had sparred for the simple joy of it. Then something changed and the boxing ring became his arena to release the ever-present tension he felt inside. Seeing this, Eric felt a pinch in his heart and a wave of sadness from his past self. The boxer had lost someone dear to him. It was after this that he had started to fight in earnest.

The young boxer had lived in a bustling port city with his wife and their son. He loved his wife, with her olive skin and the way her big dark eyes looked up at him. She had died giving birth to their second child, and the baby died soon after, leaving the boxer alone with their small son.

Eric saw a colourful city somewhere in Latin America. Crowded dusty streets were lined with weathered wooden buildings and food stalls selling bread and corn. The boxer had come to the city some years before to work on the docks, leaving his father and brothers behind on the family farm.

In the days after his wife died the bereaved man walked the busy streets with his son, going nowhere in particular. What was he going to do without his wife? He had no idea. He loved his son but he didn't have a clue about taking care of a child. With no family in the city, the young boxer didn't know where to turn. He was angry, but at nothing, or everything—he didn't know. There was no one to blame. If only this great beast of a city would be quiet and let him think.

After a while things fell into place. Some good friends took the young father and son into their family home. It was a good home but the boxer grieved for his wife. He put more and more time into his boxing, training every evening until he was tired enough to get some sleep.

Now he wanted to be the best and he fought with anger and hurt his opponents more. Fighting in the boxing ring was the only time he didn't feel lonely. He left his labouring job at the waterfront so he could devote more time to boxing.

The boxing matches, which were illegal, were held at the docks in a huge warehouse that smelled perpetually of ripe bananas and sweat. In the ring, urged on by crowds of cheering men, the boxer was completely focused. There were no rules. The opponents just fought until the first man fell and couldn't drag himself up again. The referee did little apart from making sure the opponents didn't kill each other. The police turned a blind eye so long as no one was hurt. The crowd bet on the fighters and sometimes there was a lot of money to be made.

Eric felt his past self in the boxing ring, totally centred and focused. For that short time his world went no further than the small square delineated by the ropes and the opponent facing him. Gone was the sorrow that still woke him regularly with dreams of his wife, as if she were sleeping in the bed right next to him. His anger made him strong. Everything else dropped away. It was the closest thing he knew to freedom.

For a while it was not a bad life. The boxer became more strategic in his fighting style, pacing himself and waiting for the right moment to strike. He knew how to knock down even the largest man using a series of surprise moves and he gained a reputation for winning. The crowds and the stakes grew bigger.

Years passed like this, with the boxer never thinking beyond the next fight. He hardly noticed that he was getting older and that his son was growing into a young man. Eric liked the way it felt to be that boxer. Life was hard but simple. He trained, he fought. He loved his son, he laughed with his friends. There was not much deep thinking required of him.

From time to time the boxer's son asked his father about his grandparents, uncles and cousins, and he begged to meet them. The boxer promised his boy they would make the trip together but there was always something to delay their journey: training for the next big fight or recovering from the latest minor injury.

Then one day the boxer received news that his father had died. Saddened, he wished he could have seen the old man one more time before his death. Now his teenaged son would never know his own grandfather. It was time for the boy to meet the rest of the family before it was too late.

Father and son made the long journey to the family farm. It was harvest time and the boxer knew his brothers could use the extra help. Besides, he was getting older and knew he couldn't fight forever. Perhaps it was time to change his lifestyle, and return to the fields and clean air.

After the funeral was over and life on the farm had settled back into its mellow routine, the boxer grew restless. It was so dismally quiet compared with the bustle of the city. He remembered why he had left the farm in the first place. Nothing interesting ever happened in the country. He thought about the exuberant city, where the evening air wafted food smells and music through every window and every week brought something new to talk about.

Without the boxing ring in which to vent his frustrations, the man became irritable and aggressive. Restless, he argued with his brothers and clashed with the other farm workers. Eventually, for the sake of everyone, they all agreed it would be better if he left. His son stayed to work on the farm and the boxer returned to the city alone.

He soon found work on the docks and a place to live, but the year's events had jolted him out of his routine and he was not happy. It was a long time since he had felt lonely, but now he was alone and much older. Without his son to come home to, his small rented apartment was empty and soulless. His old friends were busy with their families and young people were difficult to relate to these days. He had always been too engrossed in training and fighting to think about remarrying. Now he wondered why. It was less than a year since he had left the city but things seemed different—or maybe it was himself who had changed. His city life now seemed shallow. The middle-aged man didn't know where he fitted any more. Something had gone wrong somewhere. He wasn't sure what, but it made him angry. There was no boxing ring now to express his frustrations in and many a lonely evening was spent with only his thoughts for company.

After the session Eric was asked if he could see parallels between the boxer's life and his present one. Even though Eric's personality was quite different to that of the pugnacious boxer he nodded in recognition. Underneath his gentlemanly manner Eric often felt irritable and frustrated, however he would quickly push these things away. Somehow he was not surprised to see that his anger had been there before this lifetime.

Eric could also relate to the emptiness his boxer self had felt in later years. Sometimes he worried over the very same questions, wondering if there was a point to life that he had somehow missed.

In his next session Eric saw the aging boxer sitting on the steps of his apartment building. He was smoking a rough, hand-rolled cigarette and gazing into the street. It was a warm evening and groups of young people were walking by, laughing and flirting with each other as if there was nothing more to life than having fun.

From his steps the man who was Eric's past self could see his reflection in a cafe window across the street. He was balding, with a slightly stiff back that was a legacy from a particularly memorable fight. The distorted image in the window seemed to mirror his life. Who was he? Where was he going? Now that his boxing life was behind him, the preoccupations that had once kept him so busy had fallen away. He hadn't planned on being alone. He had never thought planning was important and had drifted through life, taking things as they came. Now he didn't fit anywhere. Where had he gone wrong? What was the point of anything? He wished life could be more simple.

Eric remembered how vital and alive the young boxer used to feel while he was fighting. Eric would have loved to feel even half that amount of vigour in his present life. There was strength in the young boxer's body, built through physical labour and daily workouts. The man's stamina reminded Eric of his own youth, when he had dabbled in fencing. Sparring used to be a lot of fun, he remembered.

Eric was asked why he had given up fencing in the first place. His answer was revealing. He said he had loved training, sparring and strategising, but even when he won he didn't like the way he felt afterwards. Once the exhilaration had faded he would be overcome by an inexplicable sadness. After a while he decided fencing was not good for him and he gave it up. Now he could see why. His post-match low moods were a repeat of the long-ago boxer's disappointment in life.

Seeing the boxer gave Eric a new perspective on himself. It felt great to get in touch with his fighting side. He could be dangerous if he wanted. Still, he wondered how to bring that into his life more. Although the fighter in Eric came out at times in his business dealings, in general he still felt anxious and unsure. Now he realised that both the angry fighter and the disillusioned worrier were already part of him as the boxer, even before he had lost his wife.

Eric's initial hunch had been right. He didn't like some of what he had seen about himself. But uncomfortable as it was, Eric felt better for seeing it. He wanted to understand these two sides and he knew he had hardly begun to scratch the surface. He looked forward to seeing more about both the worrier and the warrior in himself.

9
TRIBAL JUSTICE
Eric

Since Eric's first few sessions he had been quite irritable. His old method of coping with stress had been to pretend confidence in public and worry in private. Lately he found himself getting irritated instead. Eric wasn't sure this was much of an advance on the anxiety he had felt. The people around him were bearing the brunt of his bad humour.

Eric was asked to take notice of situations that made him angry, and to observe how he dealt with them. With great interest he applied himself to the task and soon had a list of things that frustrated him madly, from incompetent staff at work to disobedient children at home. He remembered the boxer of his last session. Eric would have liked to feel a bit more of the self-assurance that the young boxer had enjoyed in his prime.

Then Eric saw a past life that felt as though it had occurred long before the life as a boxer. In the inner space he felt a strength rising from deep within his belly. It was powerful but this time there were no angry emotions with it. The strength was simply a force: primitive, uncomplicated and invigorating.

Eric saw dense green jungle. A fierce-looking man was sitting on a high rock overlooking a small river valley. On the sandy river bank below the man's tribe was fighting another tribe for supremacy. The warriors fought with hands and spears, and the valley echoed with their wild battle screams. Eric recognised the man on the high rock as himself in another life and felt his own belly come alive as the man watched the bloody scene.

As the leader of his tribe, the man didn't take part in battles; that was the task of his warriors. But he was completely engrossed in the fighting and killing before him. On some level his warriors were part of him and he was in them, as if their weapons were his and their blows coming from his own hand. It made him feel enormously powerful. In fact experiencing the collective violence of his men inside his own belly was even more satisfying than participating in the fight himself. Merged with all the fighters, the chief was a far more formidable fighting machine than he could be alone.

As the tribal leader expected, his men were winning. Although a few from each side lay wounded or dead on the sandy battleground, the best fighters remained untouched. According to tribal law, all the survivors from the other tribe belonged to him. They would live on his land, marry into his people and fight for him next time.

Eric felt the tribal leader was pleased as he watched the battle coming to its end. He was gaining a number of excellent warriors and anticipated his next battle would be even bigger and better. The man's tribe was feared and respected by all those who lived near. Because of their powerful leader no one dared challenge them. The people were strong because their ruler was strong and each time they won a battle they grew in numbers and power.

Eric was somewhat taken aback by such unabashed enjoyment of violence. He wasn't sure he liked himself in this past life. He wanted to see what the life of the chief was like in peaceful times.

Eric saw another side to his past self. Ruthless towards his enemies, when it came to his own people he was a benevolent father. The tribe lived in a beautiful fertile valley with abundant food and a gentle climate. It was a good life. The chief cared for his people and they looked up to him with admiration and fear. Every man, woman and child knew that their leader had killed many people to be able to provide all this for them.

In the midst of his flow of vision Eric paused, confused. The raw power and natural leadership of the tribal chief made him feel fantastic—but how to reconcile such violent power with his own middle-class upbringing?

Eric was guided more deeply into the leader's life. What was he like when he was not fighting? How did it feel to be that man?

Eric instantly relaxed. He felt warm and close to Mother Earth. The tribal leader had an instinctive knowing of the land and the forces of nature. In peaceful times he would spend hours walking alone in the forested mountains or sitting motionless on the rocks above the treeline. There was a rocky ledge he liked to visit on the mountain above his valley. It was a place of special forces for him, and he felt immensely strong there. For hours he would sit still, becoming one with the power of the mountain and feeling only the subtly blissful energy that flowed through him from the land.

Eric saw that his past self would climb to his power place whenever he could. It gave him superior strength and vitality, but mostly he went there just because it felt good. While there he would pay his respects to the land and its bounty. He understood that from the land came life and power and into the land it would return.

Sometimes people would come to the leader with injury or illness and he would draw on the Earth's power for healing. He could never have explained how he did it—the healing happened through instinct and gut knowing. The chief knew how to sink his awareness deep into the mountain and let its life-giving forces pass through him. He ruled in the same instinctive way. From nature he drew the strength and wisdom he needed to rule, to kill and to heal.

Throughout the session Eric kept being drawn back to the special place on the ledge. He felt the man drinking in wisdom from the mountain, the water and the sky. Eric was asked what sort of inner life his past self had. Did his life have a spiritual dimension? How aware was he of it?

In that barbaric culture life often ended violently, either in battle or through accident. Eric saw though that death was not a cause for sorrow. Dying was a return to the Earth, a natural balance for the forces of birth and growth. The man's spiritual philosophy was simple: live in harmony with the land and the land will look after you. As long as these principles were followed and the right man was in charge, order would prevail.

In the eyes of the tribal chief there was no conflict between the need for order and the need for violence. It all came from the Earth and belonged to the cycles of nature. He trusted it completely. Among his people there was seldom any anger, sorrow or discord.

The tribal leader's land was extensive. From his sacred power place he could see far into the distance and when he sat there he could 'own' the land in a peripheral way. He knew how to hold it all in his own expanded awareness. In his instinctive way he would extend his belly energy right to the edges of his territory, encompassing the forests, their rivers and rocks, animals and people. Every bit of it was an extension of himself.

In the inner space, merged with the tribal man, Eric too felt his belly become one with nature. Letting his consciousness spread across that long-ago land, he became immersed in the experience. When it was time to come out of the inner space, Eric half expected to open his eyes and see himself tanned and muscled, holding a spear in one hand.

That wild and primitive life was a far cry from Eric's civilised present existence. Through seeing that life, he gained a first-hand appreciation of something his neat, urban lifestyle would never be able to show him. The leader's connection to the land gave him a self-assured steadiness and grounding that Eric envied. Even the boxer, with his restless anger, had not felt that. Something vital was lacking and Eric wanted to know how to get it back.

In subsequent sessions Eric saw himself before becoming chief in that life. He was a young man with coffee-coloured skin, tangled hair and wild eyes. He lived in the tribe's village, where they shared homes, food, stories and children. Eric's past self had an ability for healing and was being taught to develop it. As part of his training he would walk for weeks in the jungle, listening to nature as it revealed itself to him. He learned about healing plants, cleansing waters and sacred places.

It was on one of these walks that the young man had come across his power place. He knew immediately it was a place of mysterious forces. Dropping his spear, he sat still, letting the qualities of the rock resonate within him. The place made him dense and solid like the mountain, yet alive with the power of the forest and its creatures.

After discovering the sacred rock, the young warrior–healer grew more powerful, until one day he challenged the tribe's chief for leadership. They duelled and he won. From that day he became lord of his world. He was young and strong, revered by his people and feared by his enemies.

Eric struggled to come to terms with what he saw about this life. It seemed to him such a paradox that nurturing and violence could exist in such seeming harmony within the same person. Yet it felt so good to be that man.

What did the tribal leader's life hold for Eric? Revisiting it was not so much about working out a samskara as experiencing the way his past self had connected with the forces of life and wisdom in nature. In his unsophisticated way the tribal chief had understood those things well.

Despite the fact that none of this made sense to Eric's modern-day logic, it was having an effect on him. He felt generally more on top of things. The anxiety that had once dogged him in all aspects of his life was fading. At work he worried less and called on his sense of humour more. At home his children wanted to play games with him and hear his bedtime stories. Eric also felt closer to his wife and noticed that lately they had been laughing together a lot more.

Eric still struggled to accept the inner violence that his past life had shown him. He had never considered himself aggressive or power seeking, explaining that his business success was the result of steady hard work. Eric's confidence was growing, however, and his adventurous side had been stirred into action. He was seeing how anxiety had consistently held him back and sabotaged his good judgment. Eric was now looking at diversifying his business ventures, from providing low cost loans for ethical businesses to funding a theme park for children. His world was expanding, both within and without. He looked forward to his next session.

10
DEATH OF A TYRANT
Eric

Eric continued with regular sessions. A theme of fighting had been emerging in his past lives, first with the boxer's pugnacious style and then the tribal chief's violent power. The next past life Eric saw was a key step in his personal journey towards reclaiming his power. It was also a real adventure tale.

Again Eric experienced himself as a leader, this time of a small desert land. He felt himself as a man riding his horse ahead of his army in the dusty heat. He loved to fight and conquer. Astride his stallion he would lead the charge into battle, drunk with the smell of blood and victory. The stronger the opponents the better he liked it. Eric saw himself screaming like a madman as he slashed his sword in all directions. He would take down three opponents before the first had realised he was struck. He loved the feeling of marching triumphant into a city he was claiming for his own. It was all his for the taking.

For Eric's past self the warmongering was almost recreational. He did it for the pure enjoyment of killing and winning. When a lesser state surrendered immediately rather than be slaughtered, the warlord felt cheated and looked for somewhere else to indulge his lust for violence. The ruler's small army earned a reputation as a merciless fighting force.

Eric saw the ruler's territory grow until he had to withdraw from combat and spend more time at the strategy table instead. Thinking and planning were not his forte and he missed being in the thick of battle.

Eric felt the man's thirst for more war. There was always more land to own and more power to amass and he wanted to be lord of it all. For a while he was unbeatable and his domain prospered. Eventually, however, the unconquered lands further afield joined forces. The tyrant found himself facing two larger powers that he dare not confront. The situation infuriated him.

The warlord's glory days were over. Eric felt the man's frustration as he was forced to rely on underlings to administer his territories. He felt caged and longed to fight. Sometimes he would go out disguised at night and fight with strangers for the pure joy of laying into someone.

Eric found it difficult to accept that this bloodthirsty man was really himself in a past life. He didn't mind the exhilaration of being the ruler but Eric wasn't so sure about other aspects of his past self. Like a schoolyard bully, the man had no awareness of anyone else's needs and feelings. To him, people were disposable assets existing only to get him what he wanted. He lied and manipulated constantly. When his advisers tried to counsel him he became loud and angry, threatening them with dismissal if they disagreed. In fact, Eric realised, the realm of reason and ideas was too subtle for the man. Discussions with his council confused him. He was far more comfortable on the battlefield than sitting in tedious meetings.

What Eric was seeing seemed to be shaping up as a great plot for a boy's adventure story. He wasn't sure what to believe. It was agreed that he would let the experience unfold for the moment and look for its meaning later.

Eric saw that among the ruler's advisers was his youngest brother, the only person he listened to. The brother knew how to calm the hot-headed ruler and to explain things in plain language. The ruler hated retaining the other advisers but his brother said it was safer to keep them close than let them go their own way. The ruler knew his brother was right. He was surrounded by enemies, not only in distant lands but living in his house and dining at his table. He just didn't know who his closest enemies were.

There was another brother who governed the far reaches of the ruler's land. The ruler hadn't seen this brother for some years and he began to distrust his glowing reports. He suspected the brother was collaborating with the neighbouring lands to form a peaceful alliance and the notion infuriated him. He wanted to conquer those people, not make peace with them. There was only one solution: his brother had to be killed.

There was no one the ruler trusted to lead such an important mission. To be sure the task was done properly he would go himself. Besides, it had been too long since he had seen any adventure. However, he knew the brother would have many supporters. His murder would have to be carried out in secret.

With a small band of faithful men the tyrant left his city and travelled north. They moved under the cover of night and hid during the day. The ruler was furious that he was forced to travel like this when he wanted to rampage and slaughter. By now though he was hated by many, and enemies and spies were everywhere. Secrecy was the only way to avoid an uprising that he could no longer be sure of defeating.

When the ruler arrived in the city where his brother lived, he was taken aback to see the brother's large residence. The man had become more powerful than he had realised. Impatient for action, he ignored the suggestion to send out a reconnaissance party. Instead, he and his men watched in the shadows until the last light was extinguished and the household was quiet.

The assassins approached the house and entered unchallenged. This, he told himself, was a worrying sign. Any man who could sleep at night without guards must be very powerful. They moved silently through darkened rooms and hallways in search of the sleeping brother.

Seeing a door guarded by two armed men, the ruler smiled to himself. His brother's days were about to end. The ruler rushed at the guards and stormed into the bedroom.

To his astonishment his brother was waiting for him, dagger in hand and a grin on his face. On the bed a woman and two children started screaming as brother fought brother in the dark room. Eric's past self realised he had brought the wrong weapon. Had his brother been sleeping, his long sword would have been perfect, but when duelling in such a small space it was clumsy. The brother easily dodged his swipes and then lunged at him with his dagger. Before the ruler knew it, his brother had stabbed him and he was down.

Time slowed for the ruler as a succession of realisations came to him. His brother had been expecting him and had staged the fight on his own terms. His own men were not making a move to help him. He had been betrayed. Had the trusted brother at home seen through him that easily and sent word ahead?

The ruler looked up at his brother as the other man hacked at him with his dagger. Once they had talked about creating a united empire together. For the ruler it had been nothing but a ruse to placate his ambitious brother as he had no intention of sharing power with anyone. Now he had lost everything. Why hadn't he seen this coming? From his present-day perspective, Eric noted that the ruler had never thought of anyone but himself.

Most astounding to the ruler was the discovery of how much his brother hated him. Murdering his brother was nothing personal, it was simply a matter of political self-protection. He was taken aback to be met with such ill will.

The petty tyrant died consumed with angry regret. He rued not killing his brother long ago and he cursed ever trusting the one at home. He wondered whether, had he shared more of his spoils with them, his brothers would have remained allies in his lust for power. It was infuriating for a man in his position to die like this. As he felt his life force draining from him he was filled with rage and frustration. If there was one thing he hated it was to be powerless.

After this session Eric had to know: Was he really a petty tyrant who lived for blood? Wasn't the whole thing a bit Arabian Nights?

It was discussed with Eric that sometimes people see lives that were not their own past lives, but experiences that express their samskaras and psychological makeup in a semi-symbolic way. For Eric, seeing the tyrant was exactly what he needed in order to get in touch with aspects of himself that had no outlet in his present circumstances. Whether that life was historically accurate or not, Eric had no way of knowing. On the other hand, he was in no doubt about its relevance for him.

Eric found these insights confronting. He realised that somewhere inside he had made the decision never to engage with power or violence again. They were not to be trusted. In this life Eric had systematically avoided situations involving responsibility and authority. Now he was starting to understand why.

In the following sessions Eric saw what happened after his past tyrant-self died. As the ruler, Eric saw his own lifeless body lying on the floor of the darkened bedroom. In a moment of lucidity, the dead man was overcome with the futility of what his life had been. What good was all his conquering now? The intoxicating feeling of power was gone, along with his life force. He felt weak and confused. For the first time in decades he was afraid. He never wanted to be powerful like that again. There must be another way.

Eric continued with regular sessions and over the next few months he saw more past lives. Some were violent, others peaceful. Common to them all was the same intoxicating sense of power in his belly. Sometimes it was a primal force that wanted to rampage, and at other times it manifested as a wisdom that gave him an instinctive understanding of the land and made him stand out as a natural leader.

Along the way Eric also saw his childhood clashes with his dominating father. In this life he had been on the receiving end of tyranny, and Eric had the feeling he had been drawn to be born as his father's child not because of some kind of cosmic retribution but because they shared a similar force. However, Eric's discordant relationship with power had made him victim to his father's bullying and made him shy away from violence even more.

In all Eric's sessions there was not one that stood out as a turning point, and yet he was changing. Slowly he began to see the force in his belly as an important part of himself. As long as he remained distanced from that he could never really be himself. As Eric embraced the parts of himself that loved challenge, danger and intensity, his anxiety became a thing of the past. There was a growing quality of steadfastness and solidity about him.

At the beginning of his past-life exploration Eric had intuited he might discover things about himself he would not like. While this was true, he had also found many positive surprises. Through facing his own violence he was reclaiming his power. No longer invisible in a crowd, Eric was running his company in a completely different way. He had once told me he didn't really understand most people and felt they didn't like him. Now things were opening up for him, and he wanted to lead a winning team. Best of all, the challenge and exhilaration of leadership was bringing out a whole new side to Eric. He felt closer to his real self than he ever had.

11
JEALOUS ATTACK
Giannetta

The moment Giannetta had sat in her manager's chair behind the huge desk she had been hit by a tremendous wave of anxiety. Did she have what it took to live up to the demands of her new job?

Giannetta was a relatively recent arrival in the office and was nervous her promotion would stir up reactions among the long-term staff members. If there was jealousy she feared it would end in disaster for herself. At thirty-one, she had the experience, the ideas and the personality to be a leader, but she was held back by her own insecurity. If she could get to the bottom of that, she hoped she could make a real difference in the company.

Beginning with her concerns about the promotion, Giannetta entered the inner space. After some time she had impressions of a farm where a team of labourers were hard at work cutting hay under the warm sun. These were pre-industrial times and the men slashed the hay with long scythes. The hay was being stacked high on a cart, before being carried to the barn for winter. Giannetta was struck by the colours of the landscape: the bright gold of the hay and the blue of the wide open sky. By contrast, the farm workers were dressed in shades of faded brown, their shoulders sun-bronzed from long summer days under the sun.

At the top of the hay cart was a teenaged boy, deftly catching and stacking the bundles of hay while directing the team at the bottom. On seeing the young man Giannetta felt he was herself in a past life. She identified with something in this farm boy that was unmistakably the same as the essence of Giannetta today.

The young man put all his energy into the task at hand. Barely sixteen, he was proud to be foreman of the gang and took his responsibility seriously. He was the eldest son of the farm owner and had led a privileged life. Far from making him lazy, the boy's position had spurred him to do his best and he pushed his team to do the same.

The youth paused in his work and stood up straight, stretching his back. Scanning the sky, he noticed an afternoon shower was on its way and urged his team to work faster. Now Giannetta sensed an air of deception around the boy, although the naïve young lad was completely oblivious to it. It seemed one of the farm workers, a big man with a thick black beard, did not share the boy's good spirits. The man was the boy's uncle and he deeply resented his young nephew's promotion. The uncle never challenged the young foreman directly but in his jealousy took every opportunity to make things difficult for him.

Late one afternoon when the boy left the team in search of a forgotten pitchfork, the jealous uncle followed him unseen. When the young foreman was alone the big man lifted his pitchfork high in the air and brought it down with full force against his nephew's back. Giannetta felt a terrible pain explode in the boy's back and his legs gave way. With a cry he collapsed onto the dirt. He raised his head and saw his uncle standing there, pitchfork in his hand and a triumphant smile on his face.

Without a word the uncle reached down and grabbed the youth's hat, then turned on his heel and walked away. The boy was left lying on the ground, gasping with pain. He could hardly believe what had just happened. His uncle, whom he had always trusted as a friend, had attacked him from behind in cold blood. Dizzy with pain and unable to move his legs, the young man lay there helpless.

Reluctantly he realised he had been ignoring the signs of his uncle's growing antagonism. In years gone by the two had played ball games and fished in the river together. However, since his father had become ill and handed over the farm work to his son, the uncle had become distant and irritable. Caught up in the challenges of his new role, the young man hadn't registered what the change in his uncle's attitude had meant. Now he wished he had been more alert.

After a long time the uncle returned with another man and pretended he had just discovered his young boss lying injured on the ground. The black-bearded uncle then directed six men to carry the lad home, urging them to move gently.

The boy couldn't believe what was happening. He had lost all sensation below the waist. Terrified, he realised he might not even regain the use of his legs, let alone be able to run the family farm. Worse was the knowledge that this had happened at the hand of the uncle he had trusted.

After that day came long weeks of lying in bed with nothing to do but think. The farm work couldn't wait for anyone, so the boy's father had no choice but to put the uncle in charge. From his bed the boy tried to tell someone what had happened, but there was no one to listen. His father was too sick to care about what he called petty farm politics and everyone else thought he had imagined it.

Rather than being angry or vengeful, the young man blamed himself. The way he saw it, if he had not been so good at managing the farm he wouldn't be crippled and watching the rest of the world carry on without him. If he could go back in time he would do it all differently. He would be less ambitious and more content to follow the older men, less proud and more respectful of his workers' feelings. From his distorted viewpoint, he believed it was his own leadership ability that had broken up the family.

When she sat up after this session Giannetta looked subdued. The boy was mirroring her own fears about stepping into the role of office manager. Leadership, she reflected, is a dangerous occupation. It invites attack. So much safer to stay humble and follow orders.

Feeling she had no time to waste, Giannetta squeezed in five more sessions over the next two weeks. She was afraid that if she didn't her job might be at stake. This had to be sorted out fast.

In a following session Giannetta reconnected with the teenaged boy in his sick bed. Day after day he lay there watching the snow fall outside his window and worrying over his future. He was filled with regret over what had happened. Once he had seen his life laid out in front of him: run the family farm, marry and have sons of his own. He had even harboured a private ambition of standing for mayor one day. Now none of that would ever happen. He couldn't walk without a stick and his convalescence was dependent on the very uncle who had put him in this state.

There was something important Giannetta hadn't yet seen. She was asked to take another look at why the boy's uncle was so angry and vengeful towards him. Was it really just a matter of the boy being too good at everything, or was there something else?

Giannetta understood. The boy had been arrogant and insensitive to his uncle's situation. The uncle had lived on the farm all his life and when his brother fell ill many considered him the obvious person to become the new manager. Instead he found himself taking orders from his cocky nephew, a young upstart who knew next to nothing. Resentfully he watched the boy work and his heart hardened with jealousy. That boy had the life the uncle wanted for himself: a loving family and a prestigious future running the family business. And he had achieved it all so young.

The young farm manager had been full of ideas about efficiency and productivity. He had shown no interest in listening to the voices of experience, and the fact that something had been done a certain way for decades was to him all the more reason to change it. He loved to question the old routine and was constantly looking for new and better ways to do things.

The boy had a hat that his grandfather had given him. The hat was a symbol of his position as the third generation farmer of his family. He wore it with pride, unaware of how his arrogance was antagonising the other men on the farm. Feeling the invincible optimism of youth, he believed he was better than the older men. After all, he had been made their boss. In the end his uncle had been unable to contain his resentment and had jumped at the chance to teach the young man a lesson. This he had certainly done, mused Giannetta. The uncle had broken the boy's back and his pride, and along with it had destroyed his confidence.

Giannetta felt herself as the injured boy confined to the house. In a deep part of himself the young man resolved never to be a leader again. From then on he would choose safety and anonymity over the exhilaration of power and responsibility. This decision was to have consequences that would last beyond his life. The link to Giannetta's present circumstances was clear. Even now she was being held back by a decision made under the influence of that samskara long ago.

Most of her life Giannetta had kept herself away from positions of authority. When others praised her ability to organise she would shrink back even more. Being in charge seemed to her a recipe for trouble. She had always been mistrustful of power, both her own and other people's. The consequences of the decision she had made in that past life were still being played out in her own insecurity and lack of confidence.

Giannetta could now view authority differently. It was not power itself that was dangerous, but the way it was used. As the young farm manager she had been too inexperienced, too naïve and arrogant to command respect from those around her.

Giannetta remembered an incident that had happened when she was fourteen. She had been made captain of her school hockey team just as it was entering a state-wide tournament. Without warning her back seized up and she could hardly walk for weeks. The doctors were perplexed as to the cause and told Giannetta she must have fallen badly. Giannetta knew she hadn't, but after a few months of physiotherapy her back righted itself. By then the hockey team had another captain and Giannetta's interest moved on to other things.

Giannetta fell silent. She saw the pattern she had been caught in for lifetimes, and profound realisations were taking place. The space around her changed, becoming expansive and joyful. Giannetta felt something deep inside her unlock and a warmth spread right through her. It made her feel alive, as though a door had been opened and a fiery warmth was pouring in. A sense of magic hung in the air. Lying completely still and quiet, Giannetta saw a pool of light spreading through her, a symbol of the healing that was happening.

Over the next few weeks Giannetta continued to work through the issues her promotion had uncovered and her confidence grew markedly. Soon she was enjoying her managerial role. Learning how to be the boss was the most rewarding thing she had done in years. She wanted her staff to feel proud to belong to such a strong and motivated team. Giannetta had learned that being a successful leader was not about dominance or power, but co-operation and team building.

12
RUINED BY SCANDAL
Vivienne

In Vivienne's inner vision she saw a smoky bar where a stunning young woman sat surrounded by men. With her perfectly proportioned body and long dancer's legs she turned every head in the room. The men clustered around her were captivated by her flashing green eyes and infectious laughter. The young woman was fully aware of the effect she had on men and was enjoying it immensely.

Amused by the scene, Vivienne paused in her vision. She could feel the woman at the bar was herself in a past life, but the difference between that flamboyant creature and the Vivienne of today was enormous. Slightly built with a pale complexion and carelessly styled dark hair, Vivienne wore tight jeans, a black lace t-shirt and a serious expression.

Vivienne had decided to do some past-life sourcing after a particularly messy divorce. What had begun as an intense affair had turned into a passionate relationship and then into an exciting marriage. After only three years it had ended in a slinging match of hurt and recrimination. In retrospect, Vivienne wondered how she could have so misjudged someone whom she thought was her soulmate. Yet she still couldn't speak to him without crying afterwards. How could something so perfect have gone so wrong?

Vivienne's marriage was not the first of her relationships

to end in hurt and bitterness, and over the years she had seen various counsellors in an effort to break the pattern. She hoped that ISIS would help her free herself of this destructive cycle.

In Vivienne's vision of her past self in the bar, one particularly good-looking man stood out from the others. There was sexual chemistry between them and they were flirting outrageously. Present-day Vivienne had an uneasy sense that something was wrong, but she could feel her past self was too caught up in the moment to notice anything amiss.

The young woman was a singer and dancer who had come to the bar to join some friends after that evening's show. Vivienne sensed that this was not the woman's usual habit, but on this night she was visiting her hometown.

Vivienne was asked to see who that man in the bar was.

As she looked more closely, Vivienne's heart was jolted and she felt a surge of conflicting emotions. Her past self had really loved this man and her feelings were every bit as intense as Vivienne's feelings for her husband had been when they had first got together. He even seemed to have the same dark eyes that had burned through her. Immediately she wondered if it could be the same man. Feeling this woman's love triggered a tremendous sense of hurt and betrayal. Vivienne was asked to cast her awareness back to see what had happened to cause the hurt.

Vivienne saw that the performer had left home some years before to pursue a career on Broadway. She had worked hard and was achieving some success and popularity. Her current show was passing through her home town, and not only had the performer been looking forward to catching up with old friends, she wanted especially to meet the man she had left behind for the stage. Did he still have feelings for her?

The singer remembered the day her sweetheart had pledged to love her forever. He had urged her to come back to him as soon as she had got her dreams of the stage out of her system. He, along with many others, expected her to crawl back home after a few months, disillusioned and ready to settle down and have a family. However, the ambitious young woman knew she had what it took to make it in show business.

In the bar, the couple's flirting heated up and turned into an argument. The man insulted her. She slapped him in the face and he pushed her roughly. She stormed out of the bar and he followed. They ended up where they both wanted to be: in bed together. For the woman, their lovemaking was intense and beautiful—a reconciliation and a healing.

Vivienne felt the performer's vibrant sexuality and how she enjoyed love making. She also enjoyed using her sexuality to influence men. She knew the art of making a man feel strong and virile, and eager to go out of his way to do favours for her. She enjoyed charming men almost as much as she loved performing on stage.

Vivienne felt what it was like to be that talented and attractive young woman. The woman knew her legs were her best asset and that they had already won her several roles in Broadway shows. She also knew that her career had only just begun and that money, fame and success were just a matter of time and hard work.

Again Vivienne had the feeling something was not quite right. Despite her flamboyant stage personality and robust self-confidence, Vivienne's past self was somewhat naïve about life. It had not occurred to her that some people may not be supportive of her success. Never did she suspect she would be betrayed and brought down by someone she trusted and loved.

Vivienne felt herself as the singer walking into the bar after the second night's performance. Instead of her lover and an admiring crowd, this time she saw contempt, pity and, in some men, greed. Instantly she knew that her lover had been talking. Yesterday, to these men she had been an unattainable object of desire. Now they saw her as no better than a common tramp. Her lover had left a gift at the bar for her, but it was not the token of love she was expecting. Inside the box was a small carved knife and a gift card with the man's initial, nothing more. She understood its message too well. He was cutting the ties. The knife was saying he never wanted to see her again.

Such a betrayal was like a wound in the young woman's chest. She could hardly breathe for the pain. Alone in bed that night, she replayed the whole thing over and over in her mind. How could he do that to her? Hadn't he felt the same way she had? While she had believed they were reconciling with each other, her lover had been setting her up to destroy her.

Her public image was ruined and possibly her career along with it. The mystique surrounding her professional persona was due to the enigmatic mixture of sexuality and innocence she radiated. Until now she had always kept her affairs discrete and had appeared untouchable to her public. Now she would be branded a slut who had slept her way to Broadway. She berated herself for being so foolish. It was going to take a lot to restore her public image.

A cloud of self-hate crept over the young performer. At the same time Vivienne recognised this cloud in her present self. She hated her sexuality. Being a woman was nothing but trouble. The singer's ability to impress and manipulate men had ended in disaster. Present-day Vivienne, too, had never felt entirely comfortable with her sexuality. It had led her into several intense but destructive affairs.

Rumours and sniggers from strangers followed the singer back to Broadway. Then she was appalled to discover that she was pregnant. It was catastrophic for her career and her personal wellbeing. Despite her outward confidence, she was not emotionally robust.

In desperation the singer telephoned the man responsible. In tears she begged for his help. He barked insults and abuse through the phone, leaving her reeling with the shock. She was on her own. At her wits' end, the singer gathered her strength and went to a back-street abortionist.

Going through with the termination took every bit of courage the young woman could muster. But the aftermath was even worse than the pregnancy. Her hormones became completely erratic and she became ill and depressed. The fabulous sensuality and femininity that had been her hallmark disappeared in a fog of malaise. She was forced to stop work and went to recuperate in the country with friends.

The performer never regained her health. The beauty that had once made her famous was gone. All that remained of the exuberant person she had been were self recrimination, bitter memories and photographs. She would never bear a child. Her body ached and she was weak and tearful, always unwell and living in fear and mistrust.

Vivienne immediately recognised the relevance of the showgirl to her present life. She had unconsciously recreated the past woman's faulty relationship in almost all of the relationships in her present life. She had never been completely at ease with her sexuality, however, and had more than once felt intimidated by the very men she was attracted to. No wonder she found it difficult to build a stable relationship with a partner.

The hormonal disturbance was familiar too: Vivienne suffered from severe premenstrual symptoms. For up to two weeks every month she lived with headaches and intense emotional swings. It seemed as if her body was still living out the unfinished pregnancy of the performer's life.

In subsequent sessions Vivienne saw more about the life of the singer in the years after she was forced to leave the stage. Vivienne noticed how subdued her past self had become. The singer was now married and living in a large country house. Her husband was considerably older than her and quite wealthy. He was a conservative gentleman, kind and protective towards his young wife, often to the point of being controlling. Vivienne's past self was now only too happy to have someone else tell her what to do as she had become deeply insecure.

At first the woman tried to ignore her ill-health, but it became impossible to hide how emotionally unwell she was becoming. She would sob and scream for hours, then collapse exhausted into sleep. At night she woke from pain and nightmares, shrieking about monsters in her belly that were eating her alive.

No one, not even her husband, knew about the terminated pregnancy that had ended her career. Despite the woman's best efforts to forget, however, it seemed her body was conspiring to make her remember.

In a later session Vivienne saw the tragic end to that once-promising life. Crouched amid the fog beneath leafless trees the woman was bent over double, moaning as she rocked herself back and forth. The woman started wailing hysterically, letting out howls of anguish as she clutched at her belly. Vivienne felt the woman's anguish: something in her belly was making her hysterical. Once her greatest power, her womanliness had turned into an unbearable wound. She was in the grounds of a psychiatric institution. Tortured by her guilty secret and the hormonal complications caused by the abortion, the ruined singer had become so unbalanced she was unable to function. Hysterical outbursts like the one under the trees were the only outlet for the hell she felt inside.

During the weeks that Vivienne's sessions were focused around this past life she was experiencing bizarre dreams, all to do with babies. One night she dreamed she was a baby trapped in a mother's womb. Another time she woke up crying because she would never have a baby, even though she had never seriously thought about having one.

Vivienne described how when she was younger she used to go nightclubbing and flirt outrageously with good-looking men. She would make them believe they had a chance with her but she would never take them home. The next day she would be overcome with guilt. It made her feel unclean that she had used her sexuality to manipulate men in that way. Vivienne now had the clear sense her discomfort came directly from the singer's life. To her, sexuality had been like a curse.

Vivienne was also sure her numerous premenstrual aches and pains had their source in that past life. So far her doctor had been unable to help, apart from prescribing painkillers and suggesting pregnancy might bring a natural solution. Vivienne felt pursued by her unresolved past, just as her past self had felt in the mental institution.

In one particularly deep session Vivienne finally felt something let go deep within her. It was an unknown aspect of herself that had been holding on to the old pain. The experience began with an odd feeling of disorientation where Vivienne felt as though everything had been turned upside down. She realised she was experiencing the death of her past self. Finally, for this woman there were no more secrets to hide, no more pretending and no more pain. The relief was immense.

Vivienne was lying in the inner space with her eyes closed, one foot in the present and the other in the past life. Along with the dying woman from her past, Vivienne surrendered, bidding goodbye to her suffering body and turning towards the joyful ethereal light that was surrounding her.

In parallel with her past self, Vivienne felt the light erase from her belly the last remnants of the sadness that she had carried for so long. Vivienne cried, sad and relieved all at once. It felt so good to let it go. Silent, Vivienne allowed herself to be bathed in this spiritual light.

When the light eventually faded Vivienne described what had been happening for her in those silent minutes. She had felt her belly opening like a blossom unfolding its petals to the light of day. She felt filled with the colour and vitality of a flower and, for the first time in her life, she saw how she could enjoy being a woman. With such a treasure in her belly, she felt strong and full of life. With a belly like that, sex would be a beautiful adventure, not the minefield of conflicting emotions and desires it had always seemed.

That session was the last Vivienne saw of her life as the stage performer. Exploring it had not been easy going and had stirred up deep emotions, but Vivienne's dedication had paid off. She looked great, with glowing skin and shining eyes. Her health was markedly better than a few months earlier and she felt well enough to begin regular exercise.

With her newfound vitality, Vivienne's confidence soared. She put it all down to the shedding of emotional weight. Once full of conflict about her sexuality, she had found a new acceptance of herself and she was feeling more lovable and desirable than ever.

This new attitude showed in Vivienne's appearance too. Her habitual jeans and t-shirts were gradually supplemented by feminine dresses. She put aside her chunky jewellery and had her hair cut in a flattering style. Vivienne had always turned heads in a crowd, but now she was actually enjoying it.

Most significantly, the emotionally charged issue that had prompted Vivienne's past-life exploration was now a non-event. She was able to talk to her ex-husband without ending up in tears afterwards. There were several prospects for a new romance on the horizon and this time she was going to take it slowly. Instead of looking for her perfect soulmate and leaping into an affair, she would try to appreciate people for who they were, and to be genuine herself. She had had enough of living in her fantasies, and was ready for a real-world relationship.

13
SOULMATES AND PAST LIVES

Many people will walk in and out of your life,
but only true friends will leave footprints in your heart.
Eleanor Roosevelt

Beside me, two women were talking at the restaurant. One had just begun a new love relationship and the other was telling her, 'You're so lucky to have found him. I mean, I love my husband but he's not my *soulmate.*'

That conversation stayed with me for some time afterwards. Where did this idea of soulmates come from? My experience with clients has shown me a somewhat different view. Vivienne, for example, found disturbing similarities between the powerful attraction her past self had been caught in, and the initial dynamics between herself and her ex-husband. The man may or may not have been the same, but the dynamics between them certainly were.

Maybe once in a life people meet someone who stops them in their tracks. The dynamic between them is so compelling it feels as though they already know each other. They feel they were meant to be together. Could they have met in a previous life? Have they found their soulmate?

Behind that little word 'soulmate' lies a world of assumptions: that is that somewhere in the world there exists one person destined for each of us, someone who will make us feel loved, happy and complete. It's not clear where the concept originated. Perhaps it derives from a myth told in Plato's *Symposium*, which describes how human beings of ancient times were round, hermaphroditic creatures, each having four arms, four legs and two faces. The myth says they were strong and arrogant and began to challenge the gods, so Zeus taught them a lesson in humility by cutting them in two. Ever since, human beings have been wandering the earth searching for their lost halves.

Whatever its origin, the soulmate myth has become part of popular culture. It's tempting to believe there might be someone out there to make us feel adored and fulfilled. What is not clear, however, is how the longing for a soulmate has become entangled in the concept of past lives. Having been with someone in a past life does not guarantee happiness with them in the present, any more than being with them now can guarantee happiness in the future.

Past lives aside, however, I have observed a number of reasons for those rare but intense connections with people.

The first to consider is samskaras. The intensity of emotions around love, romance and sexuality makes it a natural arena in which samskaras will play out. Strong emotions for, and reactions about, someone can easily create the illusion of familiarity. Interactions with that person are exciting and awakening. While emotional intensity is no guarantee of having had a past-life connection with someone it is, as Vivienne discovered, a clear indication that a samskara has been triggered.

Besides samskaras, strong attraction—or its opposite—can take place in a more instinctive way. It can happen at the level of the life force, also known as 'etheric', or the *chi* of traditional Chinese medicine. One person's life force is not the same as the next. This is one reason why being with different people feels subjectively different. When there is compatibility on this level, your togetherness has harmony. It may be sexual chemistry, or it might foster ideas, creativity or healing. There is the sense of feeling incredibly alive. At the other end of the scale, disharmony on the life force level may cause you to feel inexplicable distaste or revulsion.

These are literally gut reactions: instinctive reactions to another person's vital energies. They happen independent of any thought process, although people may intellectually justify them later. When an attraction to someone is due to the deep responses of the life force there is no need to look for mystical or past-life associations. A person's life force belongs unambiguously to this life. At the beginning of each new life every baby receives it from their parents, along with the physical body. By definition, life force does not last between lives.

A third reason for those rare connections with another person is a meeting of something higher in both people. Being together triggers an awakening. Something profoundly spiritual is in the air. They want to give, to love, to inspire. They are living at the peak of themselves. It's easy to believe it is the other person who is special, or that this is 'the one' they have been waiting for.

All these things aside, it is always possible that people might meet someone they have known in a past life. Whether this means they should enter into a relationship with that person in this life is another matter altogether.

When it comes to therapy, entering into an exploration of past lives with an agenda of finding an anticipated past-life connection with a lover is treacherous ground. Like deciding on the answer before asking the question, or looking for an expected outcome, wishful thinking is not a reliable foundation for clarity. But then, love has never been known for its commonsense or objectivity.

If we greatly broaden the definition, a soulmate might be anyone whose presence touches something deep within us. Some rare meetings may be triggers for our own spiritual development, and possibly for that of the other person. That such a person may move another so deeply does not necessarily mean that they have been together in the past or are destined to be together in the future; it simply means that they resonate strongly with each other in the present. These encounters are fascinating opportunities for vision and self-knowledge.

14

A GLIMPSE BEYOND TIME

Bobby

Bobby had been sent by his girlfriend Yolanda for two sessions of past-life therapy. Impressed at the insights she had gained through her own past-life experiences, Yolanda hoped Bobby would find it just as valuable. When she was arranging the appointment, it appeared her motive was not completely unselfish as Yolanda had been trying for some time to manoeuvre Bobby into moving in with her. Bobby, however, remained elusive. Yolanda was hoping some introspection might make him realise he truly loved her and wanted the same commitment she did.

Bobby was not aware of any of this. All he knew was that his loving girlfriend had given him two past-life therapy sessions as a birthday present and he found the idea interesting enough to turn up.

A professional ski instructor for over a decade, Bobby had enjoyed a good life. He had taught on the European alps, the Canadian ski fields and the pristine mountains of New Zealand. His life was one snow-covered winter paradise, punctuated by leisurely sojourns on tropical islands where he stopped off for his dose of sun on his twice-yearly journeys between hemispheres. Three years ago Bobby had met Yolanda on top of an Austrian mountain and they had hit it off instantly. Since then they had travelled together, stopping in ski resorts where Yolanda found work in bars and restaurants while Bobby taught on the ski fields.

Bobby was a drifter and he had never given much thought to why he was with Yolanda, nor indeed why he was doing most things in his life. He had slipped into ski instructing not through choice, but because after spending years following the snow, teaching the sport seemed the obvious way to fund his lifestyle.

It was an easy life. Bobby could work all over the world and be paid for doing something he loved. Before he knew it ten years had gone by and Bobby's qualifications and bank balance were still pretty much the same as the day he had graduated from high school.

When Bobby closed his eyes and turned his awareness inwards for the session, he immediately liked the friendly darkness of the inner space. Although it felt homely and familiar, after a short time Bobby felt his heart gripped in a tight sensation he didn't like at all. The tight sensation intensified into anxiety and Bobby was projected back to the beginning of this life, when he was an unborn baby in his mother's womb.

It was not pleasant inside his mother and Bobby immediately knew why. She was young and far more interested in parties and dancing than babies and breastfeeding. The day she discovered her morning nausea was due to pregnancy she headed straight to a bar for a few drinks with a friend to 'talk it over'. Bobby's father was delighted at the news and he celebrated with every drinking friend he had, but his mother began to resent the inconvenience hugely. She would have preferred a hangover any day.

Bobby felt his mother's resentment keenly. He was immersed in it, as if it was mixed in the amniotic fluid that surrounded him. Bobby's mother did her best to ignore her swelling belly, drinking, smoking, eating and socialising just the same as she had for years. No baby was going to dictate the rules to her. The advancing pregnancy made her heavy and tired and after the first few months she couldn't pretend any longer. The unborn child was changing her body and soon it would change the rest of her life.

To Bobby, his mother's womb was unclean, uncomfortable and unwelcoming. The alcohol and tobacco coursing through his body made him feel distressed and he couldn't wait to get out of there. Bobby was born four weeks premature, which the doctors attributed to his mother's tobacco habit.

By contrast with his parents, adult Bobby was clean living. He didn't smoke or take drugs and while he was not averse to the odd glass of fine red wine, he would take a good game of squash any day over an evening spent drinking. Bobby said he detested seeing alcohol turn intelligent people into idiots. He didn't enjoy feeling intoxicated himself either. Alcohol carried too many memories of his parents' parties when he was little. He remembered how his mother would leave the party to tuck him into bed, breathing alcohol in his face and laughing too loudly. Bobby estimated that by the time he had reached school age he had already seen several hundred parties—more than enough to last him a lifetime.

In Bobby's next session he was taken back to his time before the womb so he could see why he had been born to that mother in the first place. For many people, seeing what drew them to their mother is an illuminating experience. What they perceive is usually far from the popular mythology that suggests people choose their parents and future life in full knowledge of what lies ahead. Most clients are surprised to see that the way they chose their parents was as influenced by emotional needs and samskaras as other decisions in their life.

Going to his time just before the womb, Bobby felt himself as a pinpoint of light in the inner space. Behind him was a beautiful place—he didn't see it but he knew it was beautiful—and in front of him was the womb of his mother-to-be. Bobby described himself as an infinitesimally small spark hurtling through deep space towards Earth. The spark of light was looking for a place to land; it wanted somewhere to express itself. Rather than a pre-ordained purpose awaiting him, the field was wide open. The brilliant little light that was to become Bobby had the potential to be anything.

In the space ahead Bobby saw a womb and suddenly, before he had time to decide anything, he landed into it. There was already a body waiting for him, although he could sense the mother had not realised it yet.

There seemed to be nothing particular about that womb or that mother that had attracted the spark to incarnate there. It seemed to Bobby that his mother's womb had just happened to be the first one he saw. He needed somewhere to be born, she was young and happy and that would do. Contrary to what Bobby had expected, becoming his mother's son felt quite random. The instant Bobby landed inside his mother he realised with dismay that it didn't feel good. He didn't like this place but there was no going back.

Bobby had found his mother just like he had done many other things in his life: not really choosing at all. Looking closer, however, he did see a resonance between mother and child. Bobby's mother was full of ideas that never went anywhere. Like Bobby, she drifted from one job or project to the next with no real planning. As long as she was having a good time she thought everything was just fine. Bobby had always blamed his mother for bringing him up without a sense of ambition or life direction. He was astounded to see that in fact it was the opposite. He had unconsciously been drawn to his mother for those very qualities.

Bobby was directed to return to the time when he was that tiny light travelling through space. He felt exhilarated as he felt himself moving very fast. He knew it was not a physical experience but the vast darkness he was in was a lot like outer space. He could see in this darkness, not like his normal daytime vision, but from something like starlight that was infused through the space. There was also a light that Bobby carried with him from the beautiful place he had left behind. The light suffused him and propelled him through the space like the solar wind behind a space sail. All at once Bobby saw himself simultaneously in dozens of pre-life journeys moving towards Earth, each superimposed on the other. Ahead of him were many different lives and carrying him each time was the same beautiful light.

Bobby's inner vision expanded once more, taking in the vastness of the inner space. A long line of tiny lights appeared strung out across space like an ethereal string of beads. In a flash Bobby knew that each bead represented a past life of his. It was a symbolic vision of his timeline. It was beautiful but the vision also held a message for Bobby. Despite the ever-present light surrounding him, most of Bobby's life beads were dull and colourless. The bright one lay far back in the distant past and in that instant Bobby knew he was seeing the one life that held the key to his lacklustre motivation. Way back then he had lost something essential, and he knew he was seeing this life bead now because there was a chance to get this something back.

Levity filled the inner space and spilled out into the room, making Bobby laugh for no other reason than feeling good. Bobby fell silent as, along with the vision of his timeline, he caught a glimpse of his own eternal nature. In that moment it was more real to him than his own name. He was no longer Bobby, professional ski instructor and world traveller, but an immortal spirit existing beyond time and place.

After this experience Bobby had a lot to consider. He had experienced a taste of what he could be and, all of a sudden, living to his full potential appeared more attractive than endless drifting from one snow-covered mountain to the next. Perhaps now was a good time for him to stop and think.

However when it came to his girlfriend Yolanda, Bobby's experiences were not going to encourage him to make a commitment. For the first time he was going to remain non-committal for the right reasons. It was time for Bobby to ask himself some hard questions. His years of carefree nonchalance were coming to an end. If Bobby wanted his life to mean something, it was time for him to stop drifting and follow his heart.

15
A WARRIOR'S PRIDE
Olivia

Olivia had a reputation for being easily angered. When her boss was unreasonable, her husband stubborn or her kids out of control, she would fly into a temper, blaming everyone else for whatever was wrong and shouting until she got her way. Most of the time the people in her life loved her for the energy and enthusiasm she carried, and learned to weather her tempestuous episodes. Now, however, her behaviour was starting to strain her marriage. Tired of walking on eggshells when around her, Olivia's husband was not the same jovial man she had married. The crunch came one day when he said he still loved her, but if she didn't do something about her anger and hostility he couldn't guarantee the marriage could last.

Olivia realised her husband was right. So many times she had resolved to keep her cool and after a display of temper she was always embarrassed at her behaviour. She didn't know why she found it so hard. After all, she had a good life. In the course of her employment as a community counsellor she saw plenty of people worse off than herself. She had to do something before it was too late.

At the start of the session Olivia caught fleeting impressions of tepees and bare-chested men on horses. She saw them riding through ice-blue rivers and across grassy plains. The wide, open land was exhilarating and it made Olivia feel like running and singing. Then her inner vision showed her a native American man standing alone on a hillside. Bare-chested, face to the sky and arms outstretched above him, he was screaming with the full force of his being. The tremendous power in his scream emanated from a deep sorrow within him.

The man had lost his only son. He had adored the youth with a great, full-hearted love, seeing perfection in everything the growing boy did. The pain of losing him was unbearable. The father's lone screaming was the only way he knew to express his anguish, and was the accepted way for a warrior to grieve. The man beat his chest and roared, directing his pain toward the heavens.

Only that morning the warrior's son had been out hunting with the other teenaged boys of the village. Strong and brave, the young man often won games and competitions against the other boys. On this day there was a contest to see who would return first with a prize from the hunt. Throughout the day the father thought about how he would praise his son if he won this time. But during the hunt a cliff gave way and the boy fell to his death. The other boys carried their friend's body back to the village, laying it at his father's feet.

There was no blood to be seen. The young man looked like he was sleeping. At first the strong warrior stared in shock and disbelief. This couldn't be happening. Not to his boy, not to him. He took his son in his arms, shaking him and calling out his name, praying there had been a terrible mistake. But there was no response and the body lay cold in his arms. The boy's soul had already departed.

A pit opened up in the warrior's belly as the loss hit him. He put his head back and screamed to the sky. A warrior could not cry. He plunged his fingernails into his chest and gashed his skin. That helped, but only briefly. He wished there was something to do or someone to fight. But death was an unbeatable foe.

The strong man's scream was the sign for the other tribespeople to join in the mourning. The women wailed and the men cried out and beat their chests. After some time they laid the boy's body on a bed of leaves and prepared for the ritual that would give his soul safe passage to the world of their ancestors.

Olivia saw all this in her inner vision and as she lay there with eyes closed, she felt the intensity of the long-ago warrior's rage and grief. It triggered memories of a similar loss in her own life, when her brother had died in a car accident some years before. Olivia had hated that helpless grief. Just like the Native American man, she had wished that there was something active she could do to make the pain go away.

After the session Olivia continued her reflections. In fact she felt a lot like that strong man. It had always been easier for her to get angry than to allow herself to feel hurt or sad.

In her next session Olivia was asked to see what the Native American man was like before the tragedy. The first thing Olivia felt was the love of a father for his son. Since the death of the boy's mother some years before, the man and his son had become very close. The boy adored his father and strove to make him proud in everything he did. The warrior taught his son everything he knew: how to hunt and fish, how to ride his horse at full speed through the forest and how to spear a deer at exactly the right place so the animal fell instantly and painlessly. He watched his son turning into one of the tribe's most promising hunters and fighters and his heart shone with love and pride.

Olivia's past self knew how to be a strong man but he had no idea how to cope with the pain of his loss. She saw that his culture valued bravery and nobility and it was unthinkable for him to cry in public. The only way for him to avoid this shame was to be angry.

One of the man's many cousins was a kind woman, who

understood and tried to help. A few weeks after the boy's death she saw the man sitting alone and quietly offered him food and company. He couldn't bear such softness and her caring made him so angry he wanted to hurt her. Roughly he pushed her away, making her fall backwards onto the ground. He barked at her to leave him in peace, saying he didn't need anyone's sympathy. Startled, the woman picked herself up and took a step back, just as the strong man collapsed into tears. For the first time since his son's death he was crying. The brave man needed so badly to be held like a baby, but he didn't have it in him to ask. Afraid of his anger and unsure of what to do, his gentle cousin hesitated for a long moment, then walked away.

Realising he had made a mistake, the warrior tried to call her back but no sound came from his mouth. She was gone and he was alone with his grief. He reminded himself that he was a warrior, and a warrior couldn't afford to be vulnerable. His son was gone and no one could bring him back. He had to be strong on his own.

The next time he saw his cousin she was timid and respectful, not daring to offer her help again. The warrior never mentioned his tears to her or the way he had needed her compassion. Before that day no one had seen him cry and he would make sure no one ever would again.

At first the bereaved father allowed himself to cry when he was alone. The grief and tears made him feel like a child, however, and he didn't know what to do with such vulnerability. He pushed it away as he had pushed away his cousin and as time passed the warrior closed off more and more. Most of the time he managed to avoid feeling the sadness but it never really went away. Poisoned by anger, the brave man's heart hardened and his lithe body became tense and rigid. Now his face was locked in a grimace, his jaw was rigid and his muscles tightly knotted.

Unable to find peace, the warrior would go hunting for days at a time, pushing himself to the limit of exhaustion so that he would sleep. It was a relief to sleep the whole night through without being woken by unwelcome thoughts and memories of the past.

Olivia was a warm bubbly person, not at all like the scowling warrior she was seeing as her past, and at first the relevance of that life wasn't obvious to her. As she saw more, though, the significance became clear. Just like her past self Olivia didn't like vulnerability—even her husband had never seen her cry. Mostly she was happy and fun-loving except when she flared into one of her angry outbursts.

In the ensuing sessions Olivia was encouraged to return to the warrior's grief until she learned how to feel it. Vulnerability was the biggest challenge for her. She said it demanded more courage than facing the angriest counselling client. As she got closer to the vulnerability Olivia was surprised to find that instead of feeling weak or sad, she felt liberated. Letting out the sorrow meant there was no more reason to be angry. It was good to start moving out of that bitter cycle that had turned the world into an enemy.

After working on this issue over a number of sessions, it seemed to Olivia that life was treating her differently these days. Old irritations had turned into non-events and other people seemed to be less defensive and argumentative with her. Olivia discovered that her natural directness could be softened with diplomacy, which turned out to be even more efficient than shouting at people.

Olivia's changes were also showing in her appearance. There was a tangible lightness about her now and she no longer wore the once-characteristic frown.

Best of all, her marriage was working better. Now that Olivia didn't feel compelled to win every argument and get her way in every little thing, life at home was much smoother. She had found a softer side to her nature and this was welcomed by her husband. Their time together was becoming more intimate, more fun and a lot more honest. To Olivia this, more than anything, was a sign of success. With her hostility constantly pushing people Olivia had been creating an unfriendly world for herself, one where she never achieved anything without a fight. Now she was making new friends and falling in love with her husband all over again. She liked the new way much better.

16
MARRIED TO THE ENEMY
Deborah

Deborah's description of her ex-husband was like a one-woman comedy routine. According to her he had been a lazy good-for-nothing who drank beer and watched football while the house fell into disrepair around him, so Deborah made fun of him with an endless succession of quips.

An attractive and sensual woman with an infectious sense of humour, Deborah seemed a likeable person who could have had her choice of partners. However, as soon as she spoke about men and relationships another side of her appeared. Then her sharp wit was edged with biting sarcasm and every sentence was an opportunity for a male-bashing joke. Exercise to her ex-husband meant searching around under the couch for the remote control. She would love to find a sensitive, intelligent and caring man but every man like this already had a boyfriend. Deborah was so full of cynical witticisms it was difficult to keep her on the topic of how *she* felt.

Serious for a moment, Deborah said her ex was a sweet enough guy but life with him was just horrendously boring. She had tried everything she could think of to motivate him to *do* something: play squash, go cycling with her or take up a hobby, but he always ended up back on the couch in front of the television. The only way to get him to move, Deborah couldn't resist quipping, was to grab the remote control from him and run.

Now in her early thirties, Deborah had never been with a man who really challenged her—especially in the bedroom, she lamented. She was perplexed. What perverse motivation had been making her repeat the same kind of unfulfilling relationship ever since her first boyfriend? Deborah hoped to make sure her next partner would be nothing like the man she had been married to for seven years.

In the inner space Deborah saw herself as a beautiful young Middle Eastern woman. She had the sense it was many hundreds of years ago, perhaps in ancient Persia. The young woman was wearing a long blue figure-hugging dress and matching headscarf. Her dusky skin was silky smooth and her dark eyes like velvet. Vivacious and full of life, the young woman was still unmarried and lived with her parents.

Deborah saw herself as that young woman in a library. She was with a small group of people, mostly men and two or three women, who met to read and study. It was exhilarating to be with these people. They stood for the highest human values: the love of knowledge and cultivation of integrity. They would spend hours each day engrossed in books and engaged in lively philosophical discussions.

The society to which her past self belonged was a melting pot of art, literature and science and took pride in being the cultural pinnacle of the civilised world. It was also rich in mysticism and spirituality.

Only the well-to-do could afford an education for their daughters. The young woman knew very well how fortunate she was. It was due to the grace of her father that the doors of knowledge were being opened to her. Learning with philosophers taught the young woman to value knowledge above all else and she thanked divine providence for giving her such a wise and liberal father.

Besides having a sharp and inquiring mind, Deborah's past self exuded a smouldering sensuality that men found irresistible. To males young and old she was simply gorgeous. The woman was still young and had never been with a man. She was quite unaware of the effect she had on men, a trait which only added to her allure.

In the session Deborah felt the young Persian woman's vibrant energy as if it were her own. She laughed with joy to feel the vitality coursing through her. It made her feel like jumping and dancing.

Then Deborah saw a man with her past self and felt instant revulsion. He was an important business associate of her father's and she was standing at her father's side as the two men spoke. The man was eyeing her body greedily as if it were a juicy peach. The very sight of him made her feel sick.

Although the father asked for his daughter's agreement, she was astute enough to understand that a refusal would embarrass her father and harm his business interests. This was the young woman's chance to express her gratitude for all she had received from her father. Telling herself there were many things in life more important than marrying for love, she took a deep breath and agreed to marry the man.

The man standing in front of her made her skin crawl, however, and everything about him was unsavoury, from his sallow skin to the way he ogled her. He had to be the most disgusting, lewd individual she had ever encountered. Averting her eyes, she tried to make herself invisible. While he continued to talk with her father, her husband-to-be kept staring at her, unconsciously wetting his lips in anticipation.

Deborah's vision jumped forward in time to after the wedding. Life with her new husband was every bit as bad as the young woman had feared. The man was rough and insensitive, interested only in himself and his own pleasure. A woman was a possession and he was pleased to have caught himself a particularly good one. In the session Deborah dismissed him as an uneducated lout from a cultural backwater. Her past self was accustomed to much better company. The woman's new husband was contemptuous of books and learning and quickly put a stop to his wife's visits to the library. From now on her job was to cook and clean, bear his children and give him sex on demand.

Living under the shadow of her husband, the young woman lost her joyful sensuality and retreated into herself. She would have to draw from her inner resources to survive, she told herself. The oaf she had married had taken her virginity and her freedom but he wasn't going to destroy her pure heart and the light of inner wisdom she had cultivated so carefully. She would keep it inside, locked away from view.

It was not only her intellectual nature she kept hidden. Deborah could also feel the potentially glorious sensuality of the beautiful young woman. Deep within her lay intense sexual yearnings and the potential to give and receive great pleasure, but her sleazy husband had no idea of these things, and no interest in finding out.

Nothing had prepared the young woman for this. Was her life to be a prison with this barbarian imbecile? She was not afraid of her husband but knew she had to be cautious. Simply being a man gave him a power over her that made him potentially dangerous.

Although the woman was able to hide her face and body under plain robes, her strength of character and quick mind were more difficult to conceal. Her husband found her intimidating and he couldn't bear it. He became jealous and cruel, accusing her of looking down on him. Vowing to put her in her place, he insulted and abused her, forced himself on her and degraded her in every way he could. Although deeply sad, the young woman was not easily broken.

Seeing his wife still had the better of him, the frustrated man grew more vindictive. A woman who didn't honour and respect her husband was an insult to his manhood. She was supposed to be loving, docile and obedient, not strong and wise. A man could never truly own a woman like this. He wanted to break her.

Seeing all this made Deborah fume. What a pig! She wanted to smash his stupid face in. Her sense of humour gone, Deborah was surprised at the intensity of anger that was welling up inside her.

In her next session Deborah saw the young woman overcome with rage. Her past self was kicking and screaming as a man was holding her down and raping her. Worse, her husband was looking on and ignoring her cries for help. Then the horrible realisation dawned—the man had paid her husband for this.

In the inner space Deborah was shaking with rage. She could feel the weight of the man's body on her. Over his shoulder she could see her husband's eyes. The mongrel was enjoying her distress. He had not done this for money but for spite. He wanted to bring her down. Along with her past self, Deborah was furious.

When the woman saw that her husband had set up the rape, the man on top of her became nothing. The woman was transfixed by the smug smile on her husband's face. A ball of wild rage was growing in the pit of her belly and she wanted to vomit it out all over him. Oh how good it would feel to rip his smarmy face apart. But there was not a thing she could do.

Determined not to allow her husband the satisfaction of seeing her humiliated, the young woman stopped fighting and lay still. Eye to eye, she met his gaze with contempt. A worm like him was not going to break her. Like every bully, he was a coward whose only chance for power was in brutalising others. Pathetic.

Despite her resolve, however, this incident changed the young woman. Her once joyful eyes became dull. The soft sensuality that had made her an object of male fascination vanished. She became tense and irritable. Something in her had died. She felt burdened by the injustice of the world and her powerlessness as a woman. Striving for nobility and beauty in this world meant nothing. In the end, it would always be the men who won.

Deborah could see how this samskara had translated to her current life. She had disguised her strength with manners and her anger with jokes. With dismay Deborah realised she had attracted her relationships from the shadow of this samskara. Unconsciously she had been drawn to comfort and safety above intellectual or sexual compatibility. Yet something inside Deborah remained like that young Persian woman, seething with rage and loathing. No wonder her relationships were unsatisfying and she so often wound up bored and frustrated. She had never been with a man who could reach the real Deborah as she had been trying to live without the best part of herself.

While Deborah was working on the life of the young Persian woman she had several dreams in which she would cry floods of tears, pouring them out from deep within her belly. The sobbing would wake her up and she would be surprised to find she was not crying at all. There was not one tear on the pillow and no memory of what the crying had been about. At the same time, Deborah had several wonderfully cathartic sessions, where she screamed out the hate and rage until she was hoarse. Surprisingly to her, those sessions were not exhausting but exhilarating. It felt just great to let the violent emotions go.

After some time Deborah found herself complaining less and laughing more. One day she remarked to me that she was starting to be attracted to a different type of man. Not the cuddly safe type, but men with ideas and opinions and a fire in their eyes. It was only a matter of time before she was ready to let one get close to her. More importantly, she had found a sense of self-worth that she had never known before. She was young and free, life was an adventure and she was going to live it to the fullest.

17
JILTED
Bea

For years Bea had been prone to bouts of depression, some of them lasting for weeks. Normally a chatty, social person, when the depression hit Bea would completely change, and have to drag herself through each day feeling as if there was a black cloud hanging over her head. Sometimes she couldn't turn up for work at all. Instead she would phone in sick and spend the whole day eating and sleeping in front of the television.

Bea lived alone in her modern apartment in a scenic part of the city. She was a senior administrative executive of a large department store, the same company she had worked for since leaving college sixteen years ago.

Bea arrived for her session dressed in standard business style: straight navy blue skirt, white blouse and black shoes. With her red lips, pale skin and tightly bound hair, there was nothing soft about Bea's appearance. Her manner was direct: she was depressed and wanted to feel better. Antidepressants made her feel dull and out of touch with herself. Bea didn't like them. She was looking for another way to regain the positive view and vitality she used to have.

Entering the inner space, Bea soon saw a thin old woman sitting at her window. It was herself in a time long ago. The woman was gazing at the numerous passers-by in the street.

They all streamed past without an inkling she was there, never glancing towards the wizened face hidden behind the yellowing lace curtains.

The old woman rarely budged from her seat at the window. She didn't read or knit or sew. She just sat. Life had taken its toll and she was tired. Some days even the effort of thinking was too much. The past was full of regrets and the future loomed like an empty chasm. One day at a time was all she could deal with. Letting her mind go blank, she sat watching the world go by and drifted into daydreams.

In the session Bea shifted uncomfortably and sighed. She knew that old woman's mood. It was exactly the way she felt when she was depressed. She would be heavy with a sadness she couldn't explain and immobilised by apathy.

Sometimes, despite herself, the old woman thought about the past. She remembered happier days when there had been people in her life. When her gaze fell on mothers with their children she was sad she had never had a family of her own. Seeing couples laughing together reminded her of her own loveless existence. Unable to remember even one person who had truly loved her, the old woman didn't think to ask herself who, if anyone, she had genuinely cared for. Behind her were decades of loneliness and missed opportunities and the memories made her feel cold and bitter. In the end the easiest thing to do was just to sit, and let the days and weeks turn into years.

When the old woman was forced to go out for food, she would wrap herself in an ancient grey overcoat that had once been her father's, grab her basket and shuffle down the street. With her head down and muttering to herself for courage, the old lady was an odd sight. Most people thought she was crazy and stared at her in pity and curiosity. Children called her a witch and threw pebbles at her from behind hedges.

The old woman felt acutely awkward when outside. When she was surrounded by people she felt more isolated than ever as she no longer had any idea how to relate to another human being. Considering her mad, not a soul tried to strike up a conversation with her. This was a relief, just as it was to get back to the safety and solitude of her own home.

Bea was asked to feel the old woman's heart. Although it felt hard, like a frozen shell, Bea also felt that something soft and vulnerable was hidden inside. How had the old woman's heart become so cold and brittle? Bea was asked to see.

Bea had the sense that her past self had grown up in that house. She had never married but took care of her parents in their old age and after their death stayed on in the family home alone. It was then that she began sitting at the window. Without other people in the house nothing happened, nothing changed, nothing broke the silence. At first friends and neighbours tried to support the bereaved daughter but after the first few awkward, pitying visits she ignored their knocks. Why did they come? They were just a bunch of busybodies who didn't even like her. Their forced cheerfulness irritated her and she didn't need their pity. Eventually the would-be visitors gave up and the woman preferred it like that.

After the session Bea was half shocked by what she had seen, half embarrassed. Her own life was so much like that old woman's it was scary. The setting was different but inside the feeling was exactly the same. When the depression took over, the last thing Bea wanted was to be a part of life. She let the days pass as she grew older and more lonely.

Had Bea always felt like this? She was asked if something in this life had started it.

Eight years previously Bea's last boyfriend had broken her heart and Bea had cried over him for three years. She decided love was too painful and life too difficult. She wouldn't let it happen again. And that was it, she never did.

Bea stopped going out with friends and gave excuses and apologies for everything she was invited to. She turned her home into a comfortable nest, with a huge cushioned couch and every modern appliance in her well-stocked kitchen. She watched the world through cable television and high-speed Internet.

Bea shivered to see the parallel with the past life. Had she been turning into that old woman at the window all over again?

In Bea's next session she immediately reconnected with the old woman as she sat gazing out through her window. The old woman's heart felt shrivelled and dry. Bea described it as love turned to bitterness.

What had happened to love? Bea was asked to go back and see. Was there a time in that woman's life when she had love around her?

Bea saw herself as a girl in her late teens. There was not a suggestion of depression about the young woman. She was full of life. Her brothers and sisters were much older and had married and left home. The girl grew up with her aging parents almost as an only child. The family home was a quiet place but she was happy there. She was young and her whole life lay ahead of her.

Bea saw a man, a friend of the family whom the girl had known since childhood. Although he was at least fifteen years older than her, they were good friends. As she grew up, the girl's feelings for the man turned from a childish crush to teenage infatuation. When she was about sixteen the girl had an affair with this man. Being with him made her feel strong, desirable and grown up. It wasn't quite love but it was intense, sexual and powerful. They would meet in hidden places and make love secretly and passionately. He told her she was beautiful, and different to anyone else he knew. He was her first lover and the girl was convinced she had him wrapped around her little finger. She liked it that way. In a few years' time he would certainly marry her.

Then one day after they had made love at their secret place in the nearby woods, her lover told her he had become engaged to a woman he had been courting for several months. The girl was stunned. That woman was her school teacher. She was old and she wasn't even pretty. She had nothing of the young girl's eager sexuality and sense of adventure. Hadn't this man told his young lover she was the best he had ever known? Hadn't he described their sex life as intoxicating and addictive? Their lovemaking was so exciting the girl had believed there was a kind of power in it that bound them together. How could he even think of marrying someone else?

Astounded then outraged, the girl burst into angry tears. This was not right. Crying and punching, she tried to change his mind but her tantrum only made him turn cool and distant. He tried to reassure her they would still be friends but she refused to be calmed. His patience exhausted, he called her a silly child and walked away. She was left a crumpled heap among the fallen leaves, her nose running and her eyes red from crying.

The teenager's grief was a wound from which she was sure she would never recover. What if she died from a broken heart? Then he would be sorry for what he had done to her. Never again would she pin her hopes on a man. Never would she trust another woman. Hurt and distraught, the girl withdrew from everyone and feigned illness, staying in her room for days. Her school marks plummeted and when her teacher tried to speak to her she burst into tears, calling the older woman a thieving whore. She hated the world and despised everyone. Why should other people be happy when she was not?

Over the next few sessions Bea explored this life in depth. She saw her past self's childhood, her stormy adolescence and the solitary older years. She was astounded at the parallels between that past life and her present circumstances. Just like the old woman she had been then, Bea had been withdrawing from life. Many a weekend she didn't venture out her own front door, but lived between the bed, the couch and the fridge. Sometimes she went for weeks without speaking to anyone other than the staff at work. She found it almost laughable. Although her surroundings were more comfortable than that old woman's had been, Bea had organised her life to ensure she would be on her own. Similarly, Bea also resented anyone who looked happy. Why should other people have love and happiness while she was all alone?

Regardless of what she thought, things were looking extremely hopeful for Bea. The fact that she was willing to look at herself so honestly meant there was a real chance for change. Behind the depression was loss, anger, sadness and a woman who simply wanted love.

At first it appeared a huge risk to feel the vulnerability, but as Bea found the courage to reach into her long-buried hurt and grief she understood her depression better. She described it as a twisted knot of anger, sadness and disappointment that had nowhere to go. Bea went through some profound emotional releases, surprising herself with the intensity of the grief and rage that poured out of her. After these expressive sessions she would be especially full of joy and vitality, laughing and making jokes.

As the painful emotions surfaced in her sessions, Bea felt herself coming back to life. Once grumpy and complaining, she started to soften and even smile. The blackness was lifting and she could see hope on the horizon.

When another company offered Bea a more senior position with more money, she was at first hesitant to make the change. The leader within her needed the challenge and Bea knew if she didn't do something different, nothing would change. She accepted the job.

On a personal level, Bea's acquaintances had watched in

amazement over a period of months as Bea transformed from a morose, solitary woman into a confident and outgoing one. Bea liked herself better and it showed. She was even open to the possibility of a love relationship. If love was to come her way maybe, just maybe, she would not refuse it.

18
TRAPPED IN TWISTED METAL
Joey

Before Joey would commit himself to an appointment he wanted answers to a barrage of questions. How did ISIS and past-life therapy work? Did it work on this-life traumas too? Could the technique take him to a particular slice of time that was lost to his memory? Would it help him with his post-traumatic stress disorder (PTSD)? Joey had read about samskaras and told me his PTSD was a dramatic example of how one samskara was affecting his life.

Post-traumatic stress disorder is a collection of symptoms resulting from a severe emotional trauma. Sufferers typically experience nightmares, flashbacks and fear. They are hyper-alert and easily startled. The syndrome can last indefinitely and has been observed in soldiers decades after active combat. Some of the more effective treatments for PTSD involve revisiting the incident with a therapist and talking through it again and again until the emotional intensity eventually abates. ISIS, with its emphasis on direct experience and finding the source, promised to be just what Joey was looking for.

Eighteen years before, at the age of twenty, Joey had been in a car accident. He was driving with friends to get pizza after a hot day at the beach. It was near sunset and the sky was orange. Dazzled by the sun shining straight into his eyes, an elderly driver in an oncoming car failed to see Joey's vehicle and turned suddenly in front of him. Joey's car slammed into the old man's at full speed and rolled right over the top of it. Two full rolls later the car came to rest on its roof in a ditch. Joey hadn't been wearing a seatbelt and was tossed around violently. By the time the vehicle stopped rolling Joey had hit his head badly and was unconscious. His friends had managed to crawl out but Joey was trapped. It was an hour and a half before he could be freed from the wreckage.

Joey was shaking as he related the story. Had smoking been allowed in the building, he would have grabbed a cigarette to calm his nerves. Just talking about the accident brought it all back.

Since the accident Joey hadn't driven and had let his driver's licence lapse. He also avoided being a passenger in a car whenever possible. From his home to work would have been a twenty minute drive but Joey commuted by bus and train, taking over an hour each way. He said he preferred to catch up on his reading rather than battle peak-hour traffic. However, it was far from convenient when he was called to a late meeting or had to go in on weekends. In truth, Joey knew it was fear that stopped him from driving again.

The accident haunted Joey every day of his life. The flashbacks that plagued him were not like normal memories. They were vivid images that created jolts of panic in his stomach. In each flashback Joey would relive the terrifying moment of seeing the oncoming car in the red light of sunset. Everything would hang suspended in time as the two vehicles collided. Then would come disjointed flashes of that horrendous ninety minutes when Joey had been trapped inside the car on his own.

The flashbacks happened several times a day and the accompanying panic and confusion meant he would have to stop whatever he was doing, take a deep breath and force himself to focus on the present. He was paralysed by the flashbacks and unable to stop the next one coming.

For a while Joey had been obsessed with putting together the details of what had happened. If he could make sense of the memories he hoped he might be able to heal at last. His friends' memories were confused and contradictory and Joey had never managed to see the police accident report. Now he hoped to lay the memories to rest through seeing the whole traumatic incident in the inner space.

It was explained to Joey that ISIS doesn't really work like that. Rather than an objective record of events, what he could expect to find would be a subjective record of his own experience. Joey would begin with what he had felt and let that direct the process.

Recalling the way he felt during the flashbacks was easy. The panicky feeling was never far from his awareness. Almost as soon as the session started Joey was back in the rolling car amidst crashing noise and confusion. Thrown around inside the vehicle, he prayed for help with everything he had. He didn't want to die. Then his head banged hard against something and everything went dark and quiet. It was a relief. He felt peaceful.

The next thing Joey knew, he was surrounded by chaos. There were people banging loudly on the window and yelling out to him. The sounds were blurred and Joey struggled to make sense of what they were saying. They seemed to be saying things like 'hold on', 'okay' and 'ambulance'. Sliding in and out of consciousness, Joey was confused and frightened. What were they talking about? Why were they shouting? He wished they would leave him to sleep in peace. He tried to tell them not to worry but his voice didn't seem to work. Then in a moment of clarity he realised that he was trapped. His arm was aching and his head felt like a storm cloud. Why didn't someone do something? Why weren't they getting him out of there?

When the vehicle was finally cut open and Joey was pulled out he was so disoriented and frightened that he tried to resist. There was too much light and noise and movement everywhere. He wanted to go back to that dark quiet space.

Over the next few months Joey came to regular weekly sessions. Besides the accident there were other incidents that emerged: the time he got lost in a shopping centre at age four; being bullied at school when he was ten; a broken heart at seventeen. Each experience had the same flavour of fear and disorientation as the crash. Joey joked that he seemed to be riddled with layers of fear.

Among the other events of the past, the accident kept returning. After a while Joey said his flashbacks had become different somehow and he struggled to describe what was happening. Instead of oblivion, he had the strangest sense there was something pleasant waiting for him in that quiet darkness, like a light or a friendly presence calling him. A few times this presence had been right there in front of him, just as if it was encouraging him to go towards it. Joey wanted to look further but he was afraid. What if he was seeing the light of death? If he followed it in the inner space would he die? Anxiously Joey asked what he should do.

Joey was reassured it was perfectly safe and that dying in one of these sessions would be rather extreme! There was something beautiful about that light for him to discover.

Joey was guided towards the missing ninety minutes, and asked to recall the qualities of that dark space. Knowing he was not alone this time, he cautiously immersed himself in the darkness, letting the space surround him just as it had on that day of the accident. And as Joey had intuited, the darkness was not empty. It parted like a veil, revealing a beautiful yellow-gold light. He dropped his guard and was instantly surrounded by its warmth. Soon there was yellow-gold everywhere and Joey was overjoyed. It made him feel unbelievably good. More than anything he wanted to stay there.

Joey still saw the crash scene but now there was gold superimposed over it all. It was with him inside the car as he drifted between the inner space and his normal waking consciousness. Outside the crumpled vehicle, frantic people ran around shouting while his friends sat dazed on the roadside. The traffic was banking up as drivers slowed to stare at the mangled car in the ditch. Through the traffic the ambulance was arriving and the setting sun seemed to mix with the gold light, turning everything golden-red.

Joey let himself be drawn into the peaceful darkness, holding on to his full awareness for the first time. The dark space was infused with light and he sensed a presence, something unlike anything he had ever experienced before. It made him feel loved, as though he would never be lonely again. Whether it lasted a few seconds or an hour Joey couldn't say, but in that time he caught a glimpse of infinity.

For almost the whole session Joey stayed in this golden yellow presence, hardly speaking a word. The wonderful light was bringing healing and it was best received through silence.

Afterwards Joey described what had happened. Until now, during the flashbacks he had always felt very alone in the car. This time the golden light made him momentarily forget he was trapped in the car. Inside he felt free and loved. It was the most beautiful thing Joey had ever experienced. He couldn't say why, but he was certain that light was where he would go at the end of his life. Because Joey had been close to death in the accident, he had been blessed to meet it briefly. From now on he knew it would be there behind everything he did, until one day he would meet it again in death. Joey understood that life and death were not as separate as he had thought, and he was immensely comforted by this. There were angels waiting for him and his spiritual home was hardly a breath away.

A few weeks later Joey looked like a new man. Since that momentous session the flashbacks of the accident, with their accompanying panic and confusion, had ceased completely. Joey even tried to test it by thinking about the accident but the flashbacks that had plagued him for years were simply not there. The whole thing had turned into an ordinary two-dimensional memory, with no more emotion attached to it than to a shopping list.

Joey was jubilant. The PTSD syndrome had been with him for so long that he had begun to accept it as part of who he was. Now, thoughts of the accident were tinged with the memory of that yellow-golden light and the way it had loved him.

Joey's habit of avoiding motor vehicles had gone, too. He described himself as feeling 'just fine' in a car. Revelling in his newly found freedom, he had been getting his wife to drive him everywhere he could think of. Suddenly the city and its surroundings were full of interesting places to drive and Joey wanted to go to all of them.

After years of paralysing fear Joey was itching to get his driver's licence again, and he had his eye on a new car. He had seen enough of buses and trains for a while. The PTSD was gone and it was time to look forward to all the exciting possibilities life had in store for him.

19
KARMA OR SAMSKARA?

Knowing that so many patterns of emotions and behaviour are caused by samskaras, where does this place karma? Karma frequently gets blamed for all sorts of things that are in fact due to samskaras. More than a few times I have heard laments that go something like this: 'Abandoned again! It must be my karma. What must I do to learn this lesson so I can move on?'

What if it was not karma at all, but a samskara that was causing the 'lesson' in question? With a samskara there is a way to work on the emotional pattern and resolve the issue.

An essential distinction between samskaras and karma is that samskaras are created through emotional intensity while karma is created through action. Another difference between the two is that samskaras are psychological imprints that are caused by a person's reactions and emotions, and which exist within the subconscious mind. Although they are mostly inaccessible to the ordinary mental consciousness, samskaras are an intrinsic part of us, mechanically colouring the way we see and experience the world. This is why, through deep psychotherapy techniques such as ISIS, it is possible to explore samskaras and become free from their influence.

Karma, on the other hand, is not part of a person's individual makeup. In the Indian tradition, classically karma has been seen as a principle through which the consequences of people's actions are reflected back to them from somewhere beyond the human level. Meaning literally 'deed' or 'act' in Sanskrit, karma is a universal law of cause and effect. It creates positive or negative circumstances depending on the things a person has done and the choices he or she has made. According to this view, once the forces of karma have been set in motion, there is little or nothing that can be done to avoid the consequences. This is quite a different situation from the realm of samskaras, where there is great scope for personal change and healing.

A picture emerges then of karma as a principle that is governed from somewhere high in the creation. Its workings take place in spheres so remote from the consciousness of human beings that they are inaccessible to us. No wonder some people assume that when unexpected things happen they must be on the receiving end of karma.

As an example, consider a trained assassin who hunts down and murders his target in cold blood. If the killer has no emotional investment in what he is doing the act of killing will not create a samskara for him, but his action does result in karma, as all actions do. According to the law of karma, somehow, at some future time, the repercussions of the killer's act will impact on him.

Now imagine the victim's side of that story. When the assassin's target sees an armed man stalking him in the shadows he is bound to experience a number of intense emotions. Depending on their magnitude, those emotions will leave a greater or lesser samskaric imprint in him. That imprint will become part of what shapes his attitudes and behaviour in his next life, or lives. For the victim, although existing karma might (or might not) have played a part in his being attacked, there is no new karma to speak of as he did not actively create the situation.

In this story, the killer accumulated karma through his act but did not get a samskara from it. His victim, on the other hand, gained a samskara from the attack, but no karma.

It's easy to see how samskaras can become self-perpetuating. Imagine a young girl who loses contact with her father through divorce. That loss is likely to create a samskara of abandonment, which later in life is reinforced each time a relationship ends. Afraid of being hurt again, the woman might grow increasingly guarded and mistrustful, closing off from intimacy and precipitating the end of each successive relationship. Olivia was living in just such a pattern. Her hostile attitude had been pushing people away and creating a world where she had to fight for every little thing. When Olivia worked on the samskara behind the hostility, everything started to change for her.

Of course it can always be said that it was a person's karma to have a particular samskara, and from some perspectives this would not be wrong. Theories aside, however, it is an observable fact that when people work on their samskaras their lives improve, sometimes dramatically. This doesn't fit well with a philosophy that sees karma as the cause of every event in life.

Samuel Sagan, who founded the Clairvision School, makes mention of two twentieth century teachers who held quite different views on karma: Rudolf Steiner and Sri Aurobindo. Steiner wrote an extensive twelve-volume work on the subject in which he detailed his vision on the mechanisms of karma. Sri Aurobindo also wrote about karma, with an emphasis always on following one's sense of integrity whatever the consequences. Without digressing into the respective teachings of these two visionaries, it is worth pausing long enough to note that they did not see karma in exactly the same way, nor place the same priority on it.

The mechanisms of karma are undeniably complex and difficult to fathom. However, the message I want to share here is a simple one. Not every pattern of negativity or destruction is due to karma. Many are much closer to home. This is good news. With the right tools, even the most tangled emotional and psychological knots can be straightened out. I have observed first-hand many hundreds of people who have created a better life for themselves through working on their samskaras. They have found a growing sense of inner freedom as conditioning is replaced with the clarity of their own higher awareness.

20
ANCIENT DREAMS
Frida

Looking every bit as though she had just stepped in from rounding up her horses, Frida sat down, flashed a smile and threw her hat to the floor beneath her chair. It was a few hours' drive from the farm where she worked and Frida had used the travel time to muse over what she was going to say. She wasn't even sure what her problem really was; she just knew she wanted more from life.

Frida had spent her childhood on the family horse stud but when she was twelve her father fell ill and the family was forced to sell up and move to town. Frida had hated living in a suburban house and immediately began making plans to get back to the land as soon as she could. She chose a high school that specialised in agricultural and equestrian studies, then gained a university degree in rural business management, all with the aim of owning her own farming venture some day.

At the age of twenty-seven Frida was well on her way to achieving her goal. She had plans to marry her long-term boyfriend and buy a horse stud with him. Her dream was to recreate the happiness she remembered from her childhood on the farm so she could give the same to her own children. But despite what she had achieved, Frida wasn't happy, and most days she went through the motions of work and study without any real interest or spark. 'There must be more to life', was her constant thought.

Frida was a direct, no-nonsense person. She knew her malaise must be coming from within herself but she had no idea why and she needed to get to the bottom of it.

A few weeks after beginning regular sessions, Frida experienced herself as a young woman in a long beige dress carrying a jug of water on her head. Although the woman lived in a temple complex she was not a priestess, only a temple caretaker. She daydreamed about joining the priests in their daily devotions but protocol banned her from the chapels until the last priest had left.

The temple where she lived was a beautiful place, with tall white pillars, stone floors and a silent courtyard through which warm breezes blew under blue skies. Priests in long robes walked between chapels, greeting each other as they passed.

What the cleaner loved the most was the time she had to herself in the chapels after the priests had finished their rituals. Alone she would sit basking in the silvery brightness that lingered in the space. It carried blessings from the gods that uplifted and inspired her.

At first, experiencing herself as the temple girl made Frida feel fantastic. Through her devotion the young woman lived closer to the gods she served than many of the priests did, despite their official titles and positions. In everything she did she felt the love of the Divine, whether it was praying, cleaning floors or gathering food. Her innocent devotion was her driving force towards the light.

The young woman was dissatisfied with her role in the temple and she wished she could take part in the ceremonies. Why couldn't she have been born into a family that would have given her the right to sit in that inspiring temple energy every day? Custom decreed that a temple cleaner was all she would ever be and she cursed the twist of fate that had trapped her in the wrong life.

As the years passed the young woman's aspiration and longing turned slowly to resentment until eventually her begrudging attitude distanced her from the very thing she wanted. Enmeshed in self-pity, she became impervious to the temple and its beautiful energies. All she could feel was her own discontent.

Even while feeling the temple cleaner's resentment, Frida also saw that the priests were not as praiseworthy or spiritual as her past self had believed. Many of them drifted through their prayers and ceremonies with no more spiritual aspiration than the animals in the fields. By contrast, the young woman's constant yearning had made her receptive to the light and presence of higher beings. Had she not been so preoccupied with what she couldn't have, every moment of her simple life might have been lived in joyful oneness with the spiritual forces she yearned for.

At the end of the session Frida opened her eyes and remained still for a long minute, readjusting to the twenty-first century. The longing she had felt as the young temple woman was close to her own restless wanting, except that Frida had not previously thought about it in terms of gods or spiritual light. The Frida of today just knew she wanted more meaning in her life.

Why had the young temple cleaner become so dissatisfied with her lot? Perhaps the cause lay even further back in Frida's past.

In her next session Frida followed the sense of longing back to a more distant time, before that of the temple girl. She found herself in another temple, this time as a mature woman with a striking presence. Dressed in a deep blue robe and holding a small oil lamp in her hands, she was leading a group of priestesses in a devotional offering. In a high-domed chapel, fruit, flowers and grains were laid out on the altar as they chanted praises to the bounty of the gods.

The woman had a quiet strength about her, and a wisdom born from her love of the Divine. Her role was to honour and glorify the deities of the people and to pass on her knowledge of all this to the younger priestesses under her care. The thing she most wanted to convey to her young charges was her own love of Spirit, the thing that brought meaning to life. She would take her students into hours of blissful semi-trance states just for the joy of it. Their daily practices filled the chapel with the light and presence of the gods. The space they created nourished and brought blessings to everyone who entered. Frida was tingling all over as she described the experience.

The high priestess's devotional nature led her to see divinity in everything. Bathing meant being washed by the pure deity of water and breathing was to feel Spirit flowing through her. The gods were her father, mother, lover and mentor all at once. She served them through her devotion and by sharing her sense of awe and wonder with others.

Experiencing the priestess life was a huge surprise for Frida. The vibrant joy that poured through her past self was worlds away from Frida's habitual view of spirituality, which labelled such pursuits as either religious dogma or superficial new-age babble that had nothing to offer her. She had known there was something missing from her life and it wasn't marriage, land or career. Now she was surprised to discover an aspiration to live more in tune with her spiritual nature. This sincere wanting was a spiritual experience in itself, and perhaps the most real she could have asked for.

Still the question that needed an answer was how had Frida moved from the beautiful life of that high priestess to the resentful temple cleaner that followed, and then to Frida's present existential malaise? Something must have gone wrong somewhere. In the next sessions Frida was directed towards exploring this.

Frida saw something terrible start to happen in the high priestess's temple. The spiritual light and presence that was everything to her past self began to fade. In her devotional ceremonies ominous visions would come to her of the land being devastated through volcanoes, storms and earthquakes. Her priestesses began to quarrel with each other and some of them fell sick. The unthinkable was happening. The temple had always been a place where the physical world and spiritual realms met, but now gradually the familiar and constant presence of the gods was becoming vague and distant.

At first the high priestess held tenaciously to the spiritual forces she trusted. Surely they would not desert her now? But there was no denying what was happening. The light of Spirit was fading from her world and there was nothing she could do to stop it.

It wasn't long before the priestess was living every day in heartache and she mourned for the glorious states of consciousness in which she had lived.

To Frida's past self this was unbearable, especially as, like many others who had foreseen disasters, the priestess was powerless to change what she saw. In desperation she tried in vain to cling to the world she knew.

Frida felt tremendously sad. For the first time in the sessions she cried silent tears, feeling the grief deep within her heart and the sense of devastation in her belly. Frida realised she had done exactly the same thing in this life. She had tried to hide away from change as if clinging to past memories could somehow stop the passage of time.

Frida worked on the priestess life for a few more sessions. As she felt her long-buried grief in the safe environment of therapy, a sincere spiritual aspiration began to blossom. Frida reflected on the impact of the sessions. She said it was bizarre to walk down the street right after a session and still feel the ancient priestess so tangibly. She would shop for her groceries, stop for lunch and drive out of the city as normal, but it all seemed like dreams from a paper world. Frida felt like she had left her real self in an ancient temple, thousands of years away from asphalt, air conditioning and shopping malls.

IST practitioners sometimes experience this as well. After a morning spent immersed in other people's past lives and refined states of consciousness, it can be surreal to walk outside amid the traffic, food smells and lunchtime diners. This altered perspective is a reminder that nothing and no one are quite what they seem. We truly are spiritual beings caught in a strange sojourn in this physical world.

Several sessions later Frida had a profound experience. She had been immersed in the priestess life when suddenly she was projected far above herself, both past and present. At once she saw several lives together, as if superimposed on each other. There was the temple caretaker who pined for the light, the high priestess and present-day Frida lying on the mat. The space around her became vast, like a great vaulted cathedral. Frida felt enormous and brilliant, shining like an angel.

In silence the non-physical light poured over her. Frida was an indestructible thread of light in the inner space. A shred of Spirit on its way home. Seen like this, her path was a mission that couldn't fail. Frida's light might have been hidden for a while in the murk of the world, but it could never be destroyed. The light was showing Frida a glimpse of the eternal nature of human beings.

The experience was nothing less than a grace for Frida. She would never again see herself in quite the same way. Knowing intellectually that she was an immortal soul was all very well, but from now she would know it in her heart. It was the most real thing Frida had ever felt, the missing element she had been looking for. Life's meaning was not some mythical pot of gold at the end of an ever-shifting rainbow. It was a living principle of Spirit within herself.

After that Frida took a fresh look at her ambitions. Clearly, the desire for her own farm came from the nostalgia for her happy childhood. Farm life to her implied peace and simplicity. Now that her restless semi-depression had shifted, Frida found her world expanding with new possibilities. Before committing to life on the land, she could trek the Amazon or the Andes with her fiancé, maybe even live there for a while. Or she could go back to university to study for a degree in environmental studies. Now that Frida wasn't so fixated on a rigid agenda, she wondered why she hadn't thought of these things before.

In the end Frida decided she wanted to travel, not to another country but inwards. If she had discovered so much about herself in a few weeks, what might she find if she were to keep going for a year? Her existential restlessness had shifted focus and, with it, so had her lifelong dream of owning a farm. Had it all been due to the unresolved samskara of the long-ago priestess? Before Frida locked herself into any new course of action she wanted to do everything she could to make sure her major life decisions were from free will, not buried emotions from lifetimes ago.

Frida not only felt more interested and engaged in life, she radiated enthusiasm. One friend wanted to know what new vitamin she was taking and another asked if she was in a new love affair. Frida almost said yes to the second. She had discovered her long-lost love affair with Spirit. When she felt the devotion of that long-ago priestess, something had clicked into place. Now she aspired to becoming more like her past self, always turning towards the highest aspect of herself.

21
LEFT TO DIE
Pella

Pella was a film director who was interested in making a documentary about past-life therapy. She was keen to experience the ISIS technique but, she emphasised, only in a professional capacity. She was not in need of therapy herself. Was it necessary to have a problem for past-life therapy to work? she asked.

It was explained that wanting to fix problems is definitely not the only way, or reason, to see past lives. The technique would work just fine as long as Pella was willing to stay open to whatever may surface.

On guiding Pella into the inner space there were clear impressions of a small child, scared and alone. Pella was asked what she was feeling.

She was cold and she shivered, saying that she had always been hypersensitive to the cold. She was covered with a warm blanket but it made not the slightest difference as the cold had nothing to do with room temperature. It was coming from inside and it was charged with fear. To Pella, immersed in the inner space, the distinction between fear and cold was not clear at all. The chill seemed to reach into her bones and she felt afraid.

More impressions came. Pella felt herself crouching alone in a dark place. She was freezing cold and frightened, hugging her knees against her chest and trying to keep warm. Pella had the sense she was a very small girl, perhaps three or four years old. Around her were the rough walls of a cave, lit only by a dim glow of daylight filtering in from the entrance. At the rear of the cave were the black shapes of rocks and jagged stalactites that looked to the little girl just like monsters crouching in the darkness.

The child had been brought to the cave by her father and mother. They had sat her down and firmly told her not to move away from that spot until they returned for her. The girl understood there was danger outside and had promised to wait for them in the gloomy hiding place. But it seemed they had been gone a long time. She was getting hungry and cold and those shadows were growing bigger and darker the longer she sat there.

The child tucked her head beneath her crossed arms and curled up in a tight ball. If she was very still and small perhaps the monsters wouldn't see her. She was terribly scared. What if her family never came back for her? Perhaps something awful had happened to them. Even worse, what if they had forgotten her?

The child wondered whether she should risk going outside the cave to look around, but her parents had told her to stay put and she didn't know how safe it was out there. So she sat still on the chilly rock, listening to the drip, drip of water in the darkness, and waiting, waiting.

In her mind's eye the little girl could still see the backs of her parents and other people as they had left the cave. They were a small tribe of primitive people with long tangled hair and rough clothes. The child thought about her father, a slightly stooped man with brown skin and a crooked smile. She missed him so much, needed him so badly right now. What if he were dead? The image of him and the others disappearing towards the mouth of the cave haunted her. Not one of them had given her a backward glance. It was as if they had already forgotten her.

Bravely she stood up and went towards the grey glow at the mouth of the cave. Close to the entrance she glimpsed treetops against a pale sky and was slightly reassured. At least she knew the way out. Afraid to go further, the girl returned to her spot and sat back down. Confused and frightened, she wished there was someone there to tell her what to do.

Long hours went by. Chilled to the bone and starving hungry, all the child could think about was her clan. She had images of them massacred, lying in the dirt with their heads cut off. She had seen things like that happen once before, but to strangers. She couldn't tell whether her visions were imagination or intuition.

Everything in her was hurting. Why had they left her there? How could they do that? She must have meant nothing to them. She could just die from that, feeling forgotten. How was she supposed to survive without her people? Hadn't they thought of that? They were supposed to take care of her, she was one of them. With a shudder she wondered if perhaps there was something deeply wrong with her. She was sure she had been abandoned. The little girl had never felt so frightened and alone in her whole life.

Pella knew well what it was like to feel alone and abandoned. As a small child she had clung to her mother whenever she tried to leave her at the daycare centre. Starting school had been a nightmare—she had cried for days. The fear of being left there had felt a lot like the child in the cave, Pella observed.

During the week Pella had more insights about what she had seen. Abandonment was a pattern throughout her life. Potential boyfriends who had promised to call her never did. As she waited for the calls Pella felt just like that child in the cave. Why didn't they call? What was wrong with her?

Fascinated now, Pella came for her second session. She reconnected easily with the same past life. The cold. The cave. The terrified child. The parents who left and never returned.

To the child it seemed like an aeon since that morning when she had walked into the cave holding her father's hand. Tired from cold and hunger, she saw fragments of muddled, dream-like images. They swirled around her in the dark space. Her father, with his long hair and way of looking at her that told her she was special. By his side, her mother, exhausted as she suckled the newest baby. She saw the men with their hunting spears, women carrying babies, older children running . . . glimpses of snow-peaked mountains in the distance . . . forest-filled valleys . . . deep green rivers filled with fish . . .

There were more of the horrifying visions too. These were of her people lying butchered in the sun, jackals and vultures picking at their flesh. The images grew more confused and frightening and it was hard for the little girl to tell the difference between memory and imagination. A few times there seemed to be voices calling her and footsteps approaching but then no one came. It was just the water dripping. Outside, night was falling. The blackness grew thicker and more oppressive until the child could no longer make out the dark shapes at the back of the cave. She knew the monsters were hiding in there waiting for her to go to sleep.

For a long time fear kept her awake. Eventually her eyelids began to droop and she lay down on the cold rock, too sleepy to feel scared, hungry or even cold any more. A welcome numbness took over. The little girl closed her eyes.

The darkness was dreamy and comforting. Sleep would be easy now. It would be so nice to go away from the cold cave with its shadowy threats. She relaxed a bit more and the images became more abstract and dream-like. The shadows turned to pretty colours and she felt as if she was tumbling and spinning like a feather. Then she was flying above green treetops in the warm rain, falling from the sky like a raindrop, landing softly into blue, blue water. There was the sound of birdsong amid long grass, and flowers that sang to her. Before the child could hear what they were singing, the flowers turned into stars and lit up the night with their laughter.

These images gave a clear sense that the child was no longer in her body. Was she dead, or oscillating between life and death? Pella was asked what was happening for the girl in the cave now. She turned her vision back to the cave. The little body was still there, lying curled up on the rocky floor, dead, and the girl wasn't going back to it. She was in a much better place now.

When she sat up Pella looked like a child who had just seen an angel, her eyes shining with wonder. So that's what death is like? Really? She had always thought of death as cold and barren, nothing like that joyful and welcoming experience. At some unspoken level, death and cold had always seemed inseparable to her. Now, however, she had experienced death as something beautiful, and it was easy to see her sensitivity to cold for what it was—the manifestation of a samskara. Dying of hypothermia in that cold long-ago cave had left Pella with a deeply ingrained fear of the cold.

Two weeks later Pella phoned me to say she had decided to delay the documentary. After her inner space experiences she wanted to do it all differently, with more research and a hefty special-effects budget. In the meantime she had booked into an ISIS course where she could spend a whole week exploring her past lives.

Almost in passing, Pella mentioned that she had found a new sense of calmness after her few sessions. Because she had been to the source of her deep-seated anxiety about cold, it had lost much of its intensity and was no longer creating subliminal background stress. She laughed, remembering how she had assumed past-life therapy was only for people with problems. Now she had a very different opinion. She wished she had done it long ago.

22
ADDICTION
Elaine

At the age of thirty-seven Elaine had seen a lot. A doctor, like her husband, she had spent the last ten years working for charities in Africa treating AIDS patients and running training programs in basic hygiene and nutrition. Elaine and her husband were spending a few months back home for a much-needed break before deciding whether to return for another stint in Africa.

An insightful woman, Elaine frequently had flashes of intuition about people and events in their lives. Her colleagues and friends joked that she should start charging them for psychic readings. A few times she had caught glimpses of past lives and these had made her curious about herself. Who and what had she been in the past?

Elaine's session began with a slight cramping pain in the side of her abdomen. Soon this was accompanied by the unpleasant feeling of being forced underwater. She was being drowned. The water was cold and the sensation of being pushed down was so real that at first Elaine gasped for breath. As she allowed herself to identify more with the experience she calmed down. Although she was drowning, for some reason she felt no panic. In fact Elaine had the odd feeling of being not quite there. It was like being half asleep or drugged, as if things weren't in quite the right place or the right proportions.

The water moved around her slowly, softly, as if in a dream. The woman who was Elaine's past self was not struggling. She was facing death but she could hardly feel her body.

Elaine was guided to move back a bit further in time. What had happened before the drowning? How had she gotten into this situation?

The pain in her abdomen worsened as Elaine went deeper. Soon she felt herself as a little girl, walking with her grandmother. The pair were gathering flowers and plants in a high mountain meadow. Below them the girl could see the village. From above, the sun warmed their backs.

The child loved to help her grandma. Together they collected twigs, flowers and small plants to take home to dry. The old woman was teaching her granddaughter about medicinal plants, and in the following days these herbs would become precious remedies.

Then new impressions came to Elaine. The same place. A different time. A middle-aged woman was picking sprigs of dark purple berries from a bush. Elaine recognised her as the girl, but three or four decades later.

Carefully the woman chose the ripest berries. When the basket was full she returned to a home filled with boxes, jars and books. Around the walls hung bunches of drying leaves. In the centre of the room stood a large table strewn with piles of the same purple berries in various stages of preparation.

The woman bundled the sprigs of fresh berries and hung them from the rafters. Once they were dry she would roast them and then grind them to a fine white powder. She was systematic, precise and completely preoccupied with her work. She had been making this preparation for years. Regularly she checked the bushes for ripe berries and every day she made sure her stocks of white powder were topped up. Each berry and every white grain was precious. Elaine remarked that the woman's dedication to her work bordered on obsession.

Something felt bizarre about this herbalist. Elaine was asked to see what she did with the powder. Why was it so important to her?

The powder was a strong painkiller. The woman sold it in small packets to anyone who knocked at her door. Her customers relied on it and some of them would suffer badly if she ran out. However, the reason the herbalist was obsessed with her home-made analgesic was that she was addicted to it herself.

Just a pinch of the white powder three or four times a day was all she needed to function. The powder kept an otherwise constant pain at bay and brought on a pleasant dream-like state. Sometimes a batch would turn out stronger than usual and everything would turn deliciously upside down for a few hours.

The pain in the woman's side was in the exact same spot as the cramp that Elaine had experienced at the beginning of the session. Elaine didn't remember ever feeling it before. It had started only when she had entered the inner space. What exactly did it mean?

Elaine noticed that as she immersed herself in the past-life experience, the sharp cramping in her side worsened. However if she opened her eyes and came out of the space the pain would immediately start to diminish. It was not a physical pain, but the manifestation of a samskara. The pain was also a direct link to the past life she was exploring.

In a later session Elaine saw the herbalist as a young woman, perhaps eighteen years old. Her head was covered with a bonnet as she stood in the sunshine hanging a basket of laundry on a line. Every few minutes she would drop what she was doing and double over in pain, holding her left side until the pain passed. Elaine saw her putting a small baby to bed. The same pain was there, like a knife in her side.

The baby was not hers, but the child of her employer. The young woman was a housemaid and a nanny to the child. Thanks to the powdered berries she was able to keep her job and support herself. She didn't care that over time she needed to increase her doses to keep the pain at bay. Mostly she was just thankful to have it.

There was a man in the young woman's life. He was someone she looked up to and admired—the master of the household where she worked. Arriving home from his travels he would come to the servant girl's quarters, boots still dusty from the road, and make love to her.

The girl lived for the times the man was with her. He brought colour into her mundane life. When he was home the world was an exciting place. He brought enthusiasm and laughter, along with tales of fascinating people and adventures in far-away places. Sometimes he would bring the girl a trinket he had picked up in some exotic marketplace. He would go away for weeks at a time but eventually the day would always come when he returned.

The pain in the girl's side had a lot to do with that man. She dreamed of being his wife and having his child. Instead she was servant to his wife and the child who would one day be his heir. She tried to be content with what she had, but in her was an ocean of suppressed wanting. That wanting was the real reason for the pain in her side. It never let her rest.

One night her lover brought with him an official letter with a red seal on the envelope. She knew it was bad news. He was going away for a long time, maybe forever. The servant girl couldn't bear to think this might be the last time he would visit her bed. She clung to him, drinking in the scent of him and trying to imprint his warmth into her body. When he left a few days later the girl knew she would never see him again.

It was as if the very ground had been stolen away from beneath her feet. How would she cope without him? What good could life hold for her now? The only time she could rest was after taking her herbal painkiller. In the dream world of the white powder nothing mattered.

The painkiller dulled her ability to feel but it couldn't make despair turn to happiness. The girl increased the dose until soon she was in no state to carry out her duties, and it wasn't long before her mistress sent her away to recuperate.

For the first time in her life she felt terribly alone. There had always been someone to lean on: first her grandmother and then her employer. Now the girl was simply lost. Almost delirious, she walked the long miles to her grandmother's neglected cottage. Never a strong person emotionally, it frightened her to be alone and she shivered and cried with pain and loneliness.

The young woman started to spend most of her waking hours in a drug-induced stupor, keeping her wits together just enough to prepare her next dose of the drug to which she was now completely addicted. Keeping her stocks full became her main occupation. She walked further and further into the mountains in search of the purple berries.

Things got easier when she began to cultivate the bushes herself. This allowed her to devote more time to processing the fresh berries into medicine. She sold just enough powder to buy food and kept the rest for herself.

Despite her home-made analgesic the woman was still racked with pain, both physical and emotional. She felt herself sliding into an abyss of despair but she couldn't help herself. Her clarity was gone, replaced by a cottonwool fog. Without the powder she would be invaded by nightmarish hallucinations and the insufferable pain in the side of her belly. She was trapped. Even if there had been a solution, she would not have known how to choose it.

She became a recluse, only venturing out when she had to. Even with the powder, the pain could still double her over in agony at any time. Besides, in her drug-induced daze she stumbled and slurred and the villagers thought she was drunk or mad. Giving up any attempt at normality, the herbalist let the days pass in a haze of unreality.

After this confronting session Elaine mused over the links between what she had seen and herself in the present. She had never had problems with addiction in this life but she had an abhorrence of pain. In fact this had been her motivation to work in developing countries. She wanted to do something for the suffering of those without access to treatment. Elaine could not tolerate pain in herself either, and at the first sign of a headache she would reach for the painkillers. Smiling, she remarked that she preferred to take painkillers in powder form as it was more efficient.

Elaine told me that when she was younger she had been a lot like that past-life woman. She had always looked for someone to lean on, first her parents and then her husband. It had taken years of personal work for Elaine to find her confidence. One of her recurring issues was the feeling she was alone with nothing and no one to support her.

In Elaine's next session she returned to the feeling of drowning. Underwater. Hands and feet tied. A heavy rock attached to her feet. She felt the sensation of sinking rapidly through cold water. Again there was the sense of detachment. Even when her lungs started to fill with water she didn't struggle.

Beyond caring what her customers used the powder for, the woman had been selling it to anyone who would buy. The townspeople didn't like what was happening and found a reason to have her executed. Elaine couldn't see exactly what the charge was, but she could feel their suspicion and fear. They wanted her out of the way.

When death came it was the same blurry experience that living had been. There was watery filtered light and muffled underwater sounds, mingled with hazy impressions of water flowing. Then the woman saw her limp body being pulled out of the water and realised she was dead.

In the course of the following sessions a number of things fell into place for Elaine. She realised that, contrary to what she had always believed, her avoidance of pain hadn't been due to an innate sensitivity to it. It was an expression of a samskara. Elaine had observed herself with interest at a recent visit to the dentist. She still didn't enjoy the experience, but she could see pain was just pain. It did not necessarily come with emotional suffering. Now that some of the emotion was discharged, Elaine was surprised to find herself less anxious about the pain.

Equally as important for Elaine had been feeling herself as another person in another time. The woman she had been all those centuries ago was not the Elaine of today. That woman had a different personality and a different life and yet it had been her. Elaine had seen first-hand that she had lived before. She knew she would live again. Elaine saw her life as part of a greater journey and that gave everything more meaning. If samskaras from the past could affect her now, then working to resolve those samskaras in this life must have the potential to affect her next one.

Philosophising aside, Elaine was fascinated by the new perspective her visions of the past had given her. The sense of moving away from a life ruled by samskaras and towards the light of free choice was immensely exciting.

23
RAPE AND BETRAYAL
Winnie

Winnie, a twenty-three-year-old art student, was taking a seat on the late bus home from class one evening when she realised she was being watched. Three untidy looking youths had boarded the bus and were in the back seat jostling around and laughing loudly. Winnie could feel their eyes on her. They were surely talking about her. She panicked. Moving to the front of the bus, she begged the driver to stop the bus immediately. Puzzled, the driver refused but promised to let her off at the next stop. Winnie hovered around the doors and the instant they opened she leaped to the footpath and sprinted to the refuge of a nearby hamburger place, mouth dry and heart pounding.

She stayed close to the brightly lit store until the next bus appeared, thirty minutes later. By then Winnie had eaten two hamburgers and a large fries and was halfway through a family-size block of chocolate. She was also a nervous wreck, jumping at shadows. It seemed an age before she was safely home, surrounded by her family and her things. Only then could she relax.

For the next three days Winnie did not go outside her front door, even to the mailbox. The slightest noise during the night made her start with fright. And she was eating anything and everything to stuff the panic back down. Those young men on the bus had triggered a deep terror in her and Winnie knew that she had to get help.

The fear wasn't new. Ever since she could remember Winnie had been afraid of the dark. Her childhood nights had been riddled with a multitude of unseen ghosts and monsters, and even as an adult imaginary threats still haunted her.

In Winnie's sessions she was guided back towards the origin of her terror. In the safety of the inner space she explored the maze of fears and insecurities she carried, and was gradually able to go deeper.

In one session Winnie felt a heavy weight on her body and realised with alarm that it was a person holding her down. There was a large man on top of her. He was raping her. Winnie felt she was very young, or perhaps just innocent. A simple peasant girl. The man was telling the girl to keep quiet and everything would be fine. But it didn't feel fine at all. The girl was terrified.

Winnie felt the girl's distress in her own body. All the sensations were magnified: the weight of his big male body on her, the smell of his sweat. The girl tried not to feel him penetrating her but it hurt. She wanted it to stop. He shouldn't be doing this.

To help the experience unfold Winnie was asked to see more about the man. Did the girl know him? Who was he?

The man was someone she knew and trusted. A friend of the family, the man had been like a benevolent uncle to her. He knew a girl like her would never have the opportunity to go to school so he became an informal tutor to her. The girl loved to listen as he read from his heavy books. He taught her to read and to write a few words. Sometimes they would look at the night sky together and her grown-up friend would tell her the legends behind the constellations and how ships' captains could use the stars to navigate their way across the seas.

The peasant girl had a secret place in the nearby woods. It was a semi-cave that was sheltered from the weather by a deep rocky overhang and hidden behind thick bushes. On the dry earth inside, the girl had placed an old wooden box as a table and a log for a chair. Inside the box she kept a collection of reading material: old newspapers, a prayer book, and scraps of anything interesting she came across. After her chores were done she would sneak away to her secret place and sit poring over the newspaper, trying to decipher what it said. Reading brought the girl a feeling of exultation. She was an explorer discovering a new world.

One day the man followed the girl and asked her to let him in. At first he was nice to her but then something changed in his eyes. He grabbed her by the arm and pulled her towards him. She was afraid and started to cry but he wouldn't let go. He forced himself on her, promising her if she was a good girl he would give her a new book and everything would be alright.

What was happening felt a long way from alright and she started to protest loudly. He put a hand over her mouth and easily held her down with the weight of his body. She was terrified.

The girl tried to pretend this wasn't really happening. The man hurting her had become a stranger, not the friend and mentor she had known all her life. The body she felt being penetrated by him felt unfamiliar to her. She wished she didn't have to feel it and with all her will she tried to block out what was happening. She concentrated on vanishing into the darkness inside her tightly closed eyes. It would be over soon.

After he was finished the man pretended they were friends again but the girl was shaken to the core. She could hardly believe what had just happened. In those moments her innocent optimism collapsed and she felt dirty, ugly and afraid.

As one with her past-life self, Winnie was crying as she held her hurting belly. She knew how it was to feel dirty. Sex to Winnie had always seemed a degrading, messy experience. How it was supposed to be so immensely enjoyable had always baffled her. Although never subjected to sexual abuse, Winnie had always felt vulnerable about her sexuality. She was sure every man who looked her way was a sexual predator out to steal something precious from her.

In the next few sessions Winnie returned to the past-life rape. As the peasant girl she had been too overwhelmed to feel much. Now, in the supportive inner space, Winnie was ready to venture there. It didn't take much coaxing for the pain and shock to surface. Soon it was spilling out of her in the form of cries and tears. More difficult for Winnie to feel was the anger, but when she did the fear disappeared. In her outrage Winnie no longer felt a helpless victim but a force to be reckoned with.

Winnie was amazed at finding the rage in herself. She remembered throwing tantrums as a small child and being sent to her room as punishment. Without realising exactly what she was doing, Winnie had learned to put her temper aside, getting what she wanted through being accommodating and pleasant instead. The trouble was, burying her anger hadn't made it go away—it had just made it harder to feel. Winnie was sure it had also amplified her fear. She had had enough of being a victim. It was time to find whatever was blocking her confidence.

In a later session Winnie experienced herself in a very different life. This time she was a dark-skinned woman wearing a white blouse and a colourful skirt and headscarf. She stood barefoot on the soft dirt, holding her baby boy in her arms. Three small children clung to her skirts. Like her, the children had silky black skin and tight curly hair.

At the sound of horses galloping and people shouting, the woman had rushed out of her small hut to be faced with a terrible spectacle, she stood aghast as men on horseback stormed the village. Some were torching the straw roofs while others were snatching away the male children from their mothers.

The woman's heart froze in panic as three bearded men rode up to her shouting something in a dialect she didn't understand. One of the men grabbed her baby boy right out of her arms. She clung to the child's legs, even as he screamed in pain. The man drew his scabbard and gestured that he would cut the baby in two. The horrified mother had to let go knowing that the invaders would raise him as a barbarian murderer like themselves. Distraught, she fell to the ground sobbing.

A second horseman came for the two sons who were clinging to her skirt. The mother was forced to watch helplessly as they dragged her children away kicking and screaming. In the mayhem that followed, the marauders raped the woman, set fire to her hut and rode off as suddenly as they had arrived.

Shattered, the woman was left amid the ruins with her one remaining child, a girl. Hysterically she wailed and beat the ground with her fists, clutching her small daughter and calling on the name of heaven for help. How could this happen to her? Had she done some terrible thing to deserve such a punishment? Head bowed as she sobbed into the dirt, the woman begged the forces of good for forgiveness. Winnie was crying with her.

Eventually the flood of grief subsided and the woman sat up and looked around. Her village was nothing but a cluster of charred huts and smashed pots. In the depths of her belly she knew her husband was dead. Now she was angry at the divine powers that had stood back and let the bandits take her babies and kill her people. What sort of benevolence was that? Maybe the gods of her people didn't care about humans at all.

Or perhaps whatever dark gods those wicked men served were more powerful than her own.

Shocked at herself for thinking such things, the woman tried to hush her thoughts. It was very bad to get angry at the gods and she was afraid of the consequences. She tried to push the anger away and find the good, loving person she had always been. But she had lost her husband and three sons. Nothing would ever be the same for her again.

Winnie felt an empowering rage rise up in her belly. Her past self had tried not to be angry but had suppressed something precious in herself along with the anger. It was time to reclaim it.

Winnie's next few sessions unfolded in the same vein. When she stopped caring about being 'good' she was able to let the full force of her rage fly. Afterwards she was surprised to find she felt fantastic. The high lasted for days. Not only that, the background anxiety she had always felt was lessening. Winnie's shrinking violet nature was turning into self-assurance and enthusiasm. She was jubilant. It seemed she had found the key to her confidence. As long as she remained afraid of her angry side she would stay locked in a victim role. Just like the raped peasant girl and the village woman whose children were torn from her, Winnie had had enough. If being strong meant owning her anger, then Winnie was up to the task.

Pretty soon Winnie was laughing at herself for being such a panicked chicken that night on the bus. Those rough-looking young men had probably not been interested in her at all. The whole situation had been created by her own fears.

Contrary to what she had imagined, getting in touch with her buried anger had not turned Winnie into an angry person. It had given her permission to feel what was inside her, no matter how unacceptable it might appear at first. Getting angry in therapy had opened the way for her to go forward. Winnie was through with being intimidated by imaginary dangers. Just let anyone try to scare her now, she joked. With her newly found self-assurance she might just bite them right back.

24
RAGE AGAINST LIFE
Alex

Alex was a twenty-six-year-old drifter. He dreamed of making enormous amounts of money through doing as little as possible. Alex didn't know exactly how, but he was sure the secret to effortless riches was out there and he was going to find it. He loved to talk about the expensive toys he was going to buy: a Harley Davidson motorcycle one week, ski boat the next. At the same time he bargained for a concession price, pleading poverty. This most likely was true. Alex was a paraplegic who had never had a full-time job.

Alex lived with two friends in a rented house. His income came from a disability pension and a lot of wheeling and dealing. He would buy old things for a song and resell them at a profit: outdated computers, cars that were barely roadworthy, used musical equipment. Alex wasn't about to give away any secrets but he insisted his dealings were perfectly legitimate.

Alex had been in a wheelchair ever since a water-skiing accident had paralysed him at fourteen. It hadn't stopped him from doing most of the things his friends did, though, and Alex hated anyone to feel sorry for him.

When talking about his life Alex mostly avoided direct eye contact, gazing down at the floor with a slight scowl. It hardened his blue eyes and made him look older than his years. It was easy to see he hated the world and almost certainly hated himself too. He wore bitterness like a mask, making it difficult for anyone to see the person behind it.

On first appearances Alex didn't look like someone who would go looking for therapy. Not the kind of therapy that was all about feeling, anyway. When asked why he had come Alex said only that he wanted to know about his past lives. Before enrolling in a course in it, he thought he would try a few sessions. Alex was not ready to discuss his emotional problems with someone he had only just met.

As a teenager Alex had taken a variety of drugs, mostly out of boredom. He was dismissive of the education system, saying nothing he learned at school had any relevance to the 'real' world and his school years had been a waste of time.

Alex's concept of the 'real' world, however, was different to most people's. Since leaving school he had drifted through casual jobs and even more casual relationships, never sticking with anything for longer than a few weeks. While his friends were studying or building their careers, Alex would hear about the latest get-rich-quick scheme and trade his current job in for the promise of easy money. He had sold cars, traded shares, set up mail-order businesses and joined network marketing companies. He hadn't made his first million yet. In fact he usually struggled to pay the rent. He was certain, however, that it was just a matter of striking the right money-making venture.

Alex's reckless, tough-guy attitude was not convincing. Inside that armour was a young man who felt incredibly vulnerable. Seeing it was all very well, but would Alex trust anyone to go there with him?

In the next part of the session, in the inner space, Alex was asked to feel his heart. Memories from his childhood came to him. He remembered being fiercely possessive of his mother and jealous of the attention she paid anyone else. He recalled at least one occasion when he had shoved his younger brother away from her while shouting, 'She's mine!' In the inner space,' Alex's memories were more than mental recollections. They came with the full emotional impact that Alex had felt as a child.

One particularly painful memory was of sulking in the corner after his mother reprimanded him for breaking a precious dish. To little Alex the sense of injustice was acute. He hadn't meant to break it. Why was she yelling at him? He felt something clench in his stomach as he decided not to care. Who needed her anyway, she could go and get lost along with everyone else.

In following sessions the bitterness was followed back in time, looking for when it began. In one session, Alex felt himself as a young man wearing a brown shirt and pants and high leather riding boots. He saw a sea of faces in front of him which he regarded with contempt.

It was a gathering of townspeople who had come to watch him being hanged. Realising this, Alex's past self spat disdainful words. Even in the face of death his past self wasn't afraid of such imbeciles. He was supremely sure that he was far smarter than any of them. Alex felt so much like the young man who was his past self, he could have been speaking about his life now. It wasn't for him to follow the rules like the rest of the herd. He was his own master and life was his for the taking.

Alex was asked why, if this young man was so clever, was he about to be hanged? What had led him into such a dire situation?

Alex saw his past self before the hanging. He was talking, laughing and socialising. The man loved a good time and spent most nights in bars, drinking and gambling with all sorts of people. He was a traveller, always in a different town with a new girl and a new bunch of drinking friends. On the rare occasions he found himself alone and sober he would become bored and depressed. His main aim in life was to have as much fun as possible.

The man financed his lifestyle through petty crime, mostly theft. Just before leaving a town he would steal whatever he could, gathering his booty to sell in the next location. He was quick to call his drinking companions friends, but he could not have named one person he genuinely liked or trusted. His endless new acquaintances were useful for learning about the best places to steal from, but he wasn't interested in letting anyone get too close. Mostly he used other people to help him avoid being alone.

Eventually the man's careless lifestyle caught up with him. In a hurry to leave a town one night, he had tried to steal a horse while its owner was in the bar. He got into a scuffle and in the heat of the moment he shot a man who was trying to stop him. The dying man looked up at his killer, unable to speak. The traveller felt like crying. He hadn't meant to kill anyone. He pulled himself together. It served the fool right for not minding his own business. It wasn't even his horse.

When Alex sat up after the session he was a bit abashed by the arrogance that had emerged in him. Even more confronting, he had to admit that he carried that same attitude in the present. Behind every fast cash scheme he got into was the feeling that the world owed him a living. Work was for suckers. He was too smart for that.

Alex's next sessions showed him the samskara that had led to the life of superficial socialising and petty crime. He saw himself in that same past life, this time as a young man. He lived with his wife in a small house in the city. For two happy years everything seemed to be going well. They had each other and soon their first child was on the way. Then a few months after their baby girl was born she died of a sudden illness.

Devastated, the new mother fell into depression and all her young husband's love couldn't help her. One day the young man arrived home to find his wife had killed herself. Beside himself with grief, he left the city, resolving never to return.

The young man tried not to feel the excruciating pain in his heart, but whatever he did and wherever he went the pain was always there. He remained aloof from those around him, becoming bitter and resentful of other people's happiness. He hated the world. From there he slid into a lifestyle of lies and thievery.

Losing his wife was a huge loss for the young man, however there was a feeling that the source of Alex's bitter attitude had not yet been reached. As the sessions continued Alex was asked to see when the pain in his heart had begun. Its source was some time before the death of the young man's wife.

Alex saw himself even earlier in that same life. A toddler, barely able to walk, he was playing on the floor when there was a threatening banging on the door. While his father went to answer it, his mother hid the boy in a cupboard. In urgent whispers she told him he must be very quiet, no matter what he heard.

Through a crack in the cupboard door the little boy could see soldiers pushing past his father at the door. They shouted angry words, seized his mother and father and tied them to chairs. He heard more shouting but it was the sound of his mother crying that frightened him more than anything. He couldn't see properly what was happening but he didn't move a muscle both from shock and for fear of being discovered.

Suddenly the soldiers stormed back out and it all went quiet. In his cramped hiding place the boy waited for his parents to come and get him, but they neither moved nor spoke. Eventually he climbed out of the cupboard and saw the awful thing that had happened.

His parents' bodies were slumped against each other, still tied to the chairs. Trembling the boy walked up to his father and mother, staring at the blood running from their throats. Now he understood. His parents were dead. Gone. Shocked and confused, the small child backed himself to a corner and sat down. He couldn't tear his eyes away from the lifeless forms on the chairs. Eventually the room became dark and he fell asleep. In the early hours of the morning he woke up to see the same dreadful scene. The blood had dried and his parents' dull eyes stared vacantly past him. He felt strangely numb. He didn't know what to do.

After a long day and another night on his own, a kind woman found him and took him away. Her house was full of children, most of them not her own. She seemed like a nice lady but she was too busy to mother him properly. Among the other children the boy remained a loner who never learned how to trust. The death of his parents haunted him every day of his life. He grew up unmotivated and deeply cynical. Feeling this in the inner space, Alex couldn't avoid remarking how similar that past-life boy was to himself now.

While he was looking at this past life, something beautiful happened for Alex. Although it was difficult for him to approach his own vulnerability and softness, it was much easier for him to reach it through the child of the past life. It wasn't exactly his own sadness and yet it was. Gently Alex was helped to feel the softness that lay beneath his bitter attitude and soon he found he could cry. He was amazed at the sense of relief this brought.

Alex continued with more sessions and after a few months the inner changes he was making started to show in his life. His cynical attitude softened and he started to talk about things other than socialising or making money. If his first million wasn't going to manifest quickly then he might as well do something interesting with his time. Alex toyed with a few possibilities and one day he announced that he was ceasing sessions because he wanted to travel. He had always wanted to see Russia, the country of his grandparents, and for that he would need money. Soon he found a full-time job as a sales representative for a telephone company and started working six days a week to save. He promised to send a postcard from Moscow.

About ten months later a postcard arrived from Russia. Scribbled on the back of a picture of the Kremlin was this note: 'Sometimes the things you want are different to the things you need. I thought I wanted to be strong and I found my best strength in just being myself. I learned that wherever I go and whatever I am doing, I can look inside and find that strength.'

25
STARVED FOR LOVE
Lillian

All Lillian's life she had been overweight. Cute and pudgy as a baby, she grew to be a chubby child then a cuddly teenager. Now at twenty-two she was undeniably obese. Lillian watched the figures on the scales go up and down as diet after diet failed to help.

Once she used to feel fat. Now Lillian said she didn't feel a thing. Walking along the street she would catch glimpses of her reflection in shop windows and she was always surprised to see a fat person looking back at her. Was that really her? Did she really look like that? Lillian didn't want to think about the whole hopeless issue. It only made her depressed.

Lillian was tired of feeling like a freak, however. Shopping for new clothes was an ordeal and nothing ever looked or felt good on her. She was sure no guy would look at her the way she was. When she saw other girls laughing with boys and looking great in the latest clothes, she wondered how it would feel not to always be the odd one out, not to be the fat girl for once.

Alienated by her self-image as much as by her weight, Lillian turned to food for comfort. On the route between work and home she knew every cake shop and corner store intimately. Each afternoon she would walk and eat her way home, feeling a misfit in a world of beautiful people. Lillian had to find a solution. She was locked in her body and had lost the key. Diets and doctors hadn't been able to help. She was ready for a new approach.

After her first few sessions, Lillian started to uncover an experience that was charged with emotion. It began with an impression of lying on a cold dirt floor, alone. In Lillian's belly was the same ever-present emptiness she had tried her whole life to fill with food.

Her body felt strange, it could not move properly. It was an old man's body, paralysed on one side. Lillian had a sense he was Asian. Unable to move or walk properly, he could only drag his body painstakingly across the dirt floor with his left arm and leg. It was not far across the tiny hut but getting to the door took a huge effort. Thin and weak, his body would not do what he told it. Moving about made the sores on his legs bleed and, just like Lillian, he felt trapped by his body.

Each day the old man's grandchildren brought him food. When he saw their small faces at the door he tried to talk to them, but all that came out of his mouth were weird guttural sounds. Frightened by his twisted body and strange voice, the children would put the food down quickly and scamper away. The man was left alone to struggle across the floor to the food, hoping to reach it before the rats got there.

Lillian was asked how her past self came to be alone in those abject circumstances.

The old man had not always been paralysed. It had happened suddenly, perhaps from a stroke. When they saw he would never recover full use of his body, the man's sons and daughters moved him to this small hut away from the rest of the family. In the culture's strong work ethic, anyone unable to work was a burden on the community. There was no respect or compassion as he was a shameful waste of resources. Once head of the family, the old man now brought dishonour on them all. No matter that he had worked his whole life in the rice fields to feed his family. He was helpless and the younger ones wanted him out of the way.

At first the old man was indignant. How dare his own children treat him as an outcast? However, his anger quickly turned to loneliness. All his life he had lived shoulder to shoulder with at least a dozen family members. He didn't know how to be alone. He longed for someone to sit with him, and to treat him like a human being again.

Eventually resignation set in. So his life was going to end like this—alone and freezing in this hut, lying stinking in his own filth. Even the dogs were treated better than this. Despair soon took over.

Day after endless day dragged by with nothing but memories to fill the time. The old man looked back to when his wife was still alive and their children small. It had been a bleak existence. In all those years the brightest spot he could find was the day he had married. One day of festivity and hope among the drudgery. There had been a short time of optimism before the children came. Then there seemed to be always one more mouth to feed. His life had been one of mind-numbing drabness. Even the colours of the landscape were passionless: muted grey skies hanging low over muddy rice paddies.

The land was not fertile and demanded long days of sweat and toil. The old man had worked with the young ones to eke a living from the rice paddies. There was seldom any light-heartedness among the workers. Their father's dour manner dampened all signs of laughter or fun. Now the old man saw why they had been so glad to see the end of him. He had infected everyone around him with his own misery. Still, he found his family's lack of care overwhelming. If only they would visit him, talk to him, tell him the news. A bath would be heaven.

Lillian couldn't help noting how ironic it was that in

his loneliness, the old man was feeling more emotion than during most of his deadened existence. In his yearning for human warmth he realised he had never really felt warmth towards others. When he lived among other people he had been surly and introverted. Now it was too late. His best hope was that death would come speedily. The old man was filled with anguish. He was paralysed, not sick. He might go on like this for years, like a prisoner waiting to die. There must be some way out.

Slowly the awful solution dawned on him. Self starvation would be his escape from the nightmare. In fact, it was the only honourable thing to do. He realised his family expected it. It was his duty to make this shameful situation as short and painless as possible for all.

Next time the children brought him food the old man didn't budge from his cot. Even though the cold and hunger gnawed at his belly, he lay still and watched from his bed as the rats gorged themselves on the bowl of freshly cooked rice. After a few days the hunger started to abate, replaced by a hollownes that sucked at his insides and intensified the cold. The old man was afraid to die but even worse was the prospect of living for years like this.

After this session Lillian sat up wanting to head straight for the nearest Italian restaurant. She found the incongruity of it almost funny. That old man was well-known to her. Even as her own waistline bulged out of control, Lillian felt empty and cold inside, just like the starving man. No matter how full, she stuffed herself with food. That hollow sensation never went away, except when she was momentarily distracted by actually putting food in her mouth. Diets only made the sense of starvation worsen and over the years Lillian had grown steadily bigger.

The worst thing about her size was the isolation it created. Wherever she went Lillian felt people staring at her and it wasn't with admiration. When caring friends or family members mentioned her weight she would be deeply cut by their remarks. Sometimes it got too much to bear and Lillian would find herself in front of the refrigerator yet again, yesterday's leftover cheesecake in her hand. Just like the dying man of her past life, Lillian was desperate to escape the emptiness.

Lillian's next session revealed more about her past self. The man had closed off from his family long before they had relegated him to life alone in the squalid little hut. When he was small boy his parents had died, and he had been raised by his uncles and aunts. Although they had fed and clothed the child, he was put to work in the fields as soon as he was old enough. He had no memories of being held in anyone's arms and sung to, as he had seen some mothers doing with their babies. He had learned to survive without affection and to take care of himself, but he grew to a man knowing nothing about softness or love.

Overwhelmed by his own misery, the old man lay curled up on his bed like a child, waiting for death to find him. Enough of the memories, he was tired of life. Oblivion was what he yearned for. He hoped death would bring an end to his living hell.

In the inner space, Lillian felt the old man's wizened body as if it was her own lying there cold and filthy in a foetal position. His leathery skin was stretched taut over brittle bones, like a piece of dried meat. There was a cavernous emptiness in his belly and a worse one in his heart.

The old man felt death taking him and he waited for the relief that must surely come. But something was wrong. He knew he must not be in his body because the pain and hunger were gone, however he felt just as empty and cold as ever. The icy void in which he had been existing was also inside his heart.

In the session Lillian sighed. From her semi-objective

standpoint she could see a welcoming light around the old man as he passed over. He was surrounded by its softness but his shrivelled heart remained closed. It had been decades since he felt warmth and he had forgotten how. Lillian cried as she saw the old man's death, and saw his chance to thaw out some of the frost inside going unnoticed.

After this sad session Lillian talked about the emptiness in her present life. She remembered being a little girl with her family in the living room, warm and well fed yet feeling terribly isolated. No amount of food or heating was ever enough to thaw out that hunger and cold.

A number of realisations started to fall into place for Lillian. She started to feel the old paralysed man behind her constant compulsion to eat. His starving body and longing for human warmth were her own. In her following sessions Lillian returned to the old man's childhood. She experienced the loss of his parents and felt the child's grief that had been buried since then. As she worked on this samskara, forgotten parts of Lillian began reviving. Soon the effects of her sessions began to spill over into her life.

Lillian started exercising and marvelled that it could feel so good to move her body. Running and walking warmed and enlivened her. Amazingly, it felt better than pizza. Junk food had never filled the hollowness anyway. The more she exercised the more her body asked for things such as water, carrots and fruit.

After Lillian worked on her starvation-related samskara she was considerably less obsessive about food, but it was still a challenge to curb her eating. Lillian admitted she had been half hoping that the deep work in the sessions would magically make her thin. When this didn't happen she had to face it: samskaras or not, losing weight takes effort.

Even though Lillian had worked through an intense samskara and let go of some heavy emotional baggage, she still needed to change her eating habits and exercise in earnest to become the slim attractive woman she wanted to be. To Lillian, the most exciting result of her sessions was that she was now ready for the challenge. Inside, she felt tonnes lighter. She was determined it wouldn't be long before it showed on the outside too.

Lillian knew she still had a long way to go but she was excited to have made the first step. She had the key and was on her way towards a new body and a new life.

26
EXPERIENCES OF DEATH

Among their visions of samskaras and past lives, it is not unusual for people to see past deaths and the time immediately after dying.

In ISIS sessions people see all sorts of past deaths, from peaceful to traumatic. In almost every instance, immediately after dying they experience a period of lingering around familiar places or people. During this time their newly dead past selves see, feel and think almost as if they were still alive. They may not even realise yet they have passed over. Gradually the awareness of earthly things becomes increasingly distorted and dream-like until it fades altogether. The inner space is filled with a welcoming light and presence, embracing the dead and taking them into higher realms. There is always a point beyond which clients do not see because their past selves have gone beyond the visible reaches of their earthly standpoint.

Following are some examples to illustrate this.

During a session, Luke saw himself as a man on horseback galloping through a dark forest. The night air was chilly and the man wrapped his cloak more tightly around him for warmth. He was on a mission to deliver a message and knew the forest was no place to dawdle at night.

Suddenly the horse stumbled and threw its rider to the ground. Stunned, the traveller sat up to see his horse had bolted and two shadowy figures were emerging from the trees with knives in hand. The next thing Luke saw was the same man walking along the road. He was slightly disoriented but determined to keep moving. The mission was the only thing on his mind. The message he was carrying contained critical military information and it was imperative that it reach its destination.

Then it was daylight and the messenger had arrived at an army camp near the edge of the forest. A large man in a red uniform was anxiously pacing to and fro in his tent as he waited for the message. Once inside the tent the messenger tried to deliver his message but, bizzarrely, the officer continued pacing about and muttering to himself. Disconcerted and confused, the messenger couldn't fathom what was wrong. He followed the officer around the small space, becoming increasingly agitated and frustrated. He stood in front of the man and shouted. He thumped his fist on the makeshift desk and he called out the officer's name. At that, the officer turned towards him and started in fright. Puzzled, the officer wondered for a moment whether he was seeing a ghost. Then, shaking his head, he went back to what he was doing.

At that moment Luke's past self realised he was dead. The strangeness of the last few hours started to make sense. He remembered the attack in the forest and instantly he was back there. Floating somewhere above the scene, he now saw his body lying on the ground, his throat slit and his knapsack gone. He thought of his mother and suddenly he was in her home. It all felt so normal and yet so strange. He could still walk and see and think. If he was dead then why was he still here? What was he supposed to do next?

That was when the man noticed a light around him and

gratefully, he turned towards it. Then he was gone and Luke felt himself immersed in the beautiful light of death.

When Nina tried to go back further than her birth she became filled with anger. At the same time she saw confusing scenes of fire, blood and twisted metal. There was the sound of fire and people screaming. Her body was crushed among the broken, burning wreckage of a train crash. She was dying. Outraged, she fought against death with all her force. It was not her time to die. She was a young and beautiful teenaged girl whose whole life lay ahead. Fate was cheating her.

Nina didn't see any post-death letting go, nor any beautiful light or presence. There was just blood, fire and anger, then suddenly she was a baby again, furious to be starting over in another mother's womb. Present-day Nina had been angry her whole life without knowing why. She had brought the anger with her from her previous death.

In one session after another, Zoe saw a scene in which she was flying above trees and gardens, then a beach. It was apparent that Zoe's past self had died but hadn't yet realised it. Zoe was asked all sorts of questions to help her see what was happening but she remained stubbornly confused. Eventually she was asked directly, 'Do you think you could be dead?' Zoe was adamant this was impossible. She could feel her body, she could move and see and feel. This couldn't be death because she didn't *feel* dead.

To break the cycle of stuckness the suggestion was put that 'Perhaps that's what dead feels like.' Hearing this, Zoe collapsed into floods of tears. Reluctantly, she acknowledged that her past self had indeed died, but hadn't wanted to see it. She was clinging desperately to something or someone she didn't want to leave, resisting death with all her will. As Zoe felt the grief of her past self, the rest of the experience unfolded. Finally she was able to open to the light and find peace.

While it is not uncommon to see the first stages of a previous after-life journey, penetrating further into the mysteries between death and rebirth is more difficult. Traditional Buddhist and Hindu texts discuss how a person's state at the time of passing over the threshold has an enormous influence over where they go in their immediate after-life journey. In *Death, the Great Journey*, a comprehensive modern-day exploration of death and the after-death journey, Samuel Sagan relates a Buddhist story about this. The story is of a dying man who has led a good life, but as he lies on his deathbed he sees the greed in his relatives who sit with him. When he dies he does not pass over into welcoming spiritual light. Instead he is drawn to violent angry spaces—all because he became angry right at the crucial time of transition.

At first impression this may seem unfair, however it is simply a matter of cause and effect. In fact the same mechanism occurs when falling asleep. Just as the nature of one's pre-sleep activities can affect dream content, so it affects the depth and quality of sleep throughout the night. Your sleep is clearly different according to whether you have spent the evening watching action movies, arguing with a loved one or worrying about finances.

This mechanism was at play with Jade when she experienced herself as the woman shot by the Nazi soldier. Immediately after she died, her first concern was still the welfare of her children. Pella, on the other hand, as the small girl dying in the cave, felt herself pass over easily into welcoming spaces. Her transition was facilitated by her childlike openness and by not clinging to the things of that life. The following two chapters provide more examples of how afterlife journeys are influenced by a person's state at death.

For most people, experiences of the time after death, and also of the time just before incarnating into a new baby's body, are precious. They unfold an unmistakable firsthand knowing of consciousness beyond the current life. To know oneself as an immortal spirit existing through time is all very well in theory, but to know it through direct experience can be life changing.

27
DEATH ON THE VOLCANO
Dominic

Dominic was a forty-three-year-old company director in the media industry. Astute and well connected, he knew all the right people and was regularly seen at A-list parties rubbing shoulders with celebrities. He was a complex and sophisticated man who had a great interest in the esoteric, which he kept private from his public persona. Dominic described himself as 'too busy for emotional problems' but he had a keen desire to become the best person he possibly could. He wanted to see what past-life therapy would reveal about him.

During his first few sessions Dominic saw images of a mountainous island bordered with white sand and blue–green waves—but this small paradise was being shattered by an erupting volcano. Dominic was a woman standing on a rocky outlook, transfixed by the terrifying vision. The island was literally blowing apart, bringing an end to the woman's world.

The woman had been walking and gathering a few nuts and berries as she went. Suddenly there was an ominous rumble and the ground shuddered. Life on a volcanic island had its share of earth tremors but this was different. Alarmed, the woman stopped and listened. There was an eerie stillness. The birds had gone quiet and not even a breeze rustled the palm fronds. The island was holding its breath. The woman suddenly wished she hadn't wandered so far from her village.

Heart pounding, she climbed some rocks to see better. To one side was the familiar treetop vista across to her village at the edge of the glittering sea; but on the other side a torrent of black smoke was issuing from the mouth of the volcano. It was nothing like the white wisps that sometimes floated from the summit and mingled with the clouds. The island beliefs were about the fire and magic of the volcano goddess, not her anger. The woman felt a deep dread.

The mountain gave a terrible shudder and the plume of black smoke thickened. Fine ash started falling on the woman's brown skin, but she hardly noticed the tiny sparks burning her. Ash blotted out the sun and turned the sea grey. In the distance tiny figures were running about. Some scrambled towards the fishing boats while others were still trying to save their thatched roofs from the rain of hot ash.

Aghast, Dominic's past self stared. There was a deafening boom and the main cone of the volcano suddenly exploded. Massive chunks of rock were hurled into the sky. A rock landed on the path nearby, starting a fire and blocking the way down. It made no difference, the woman was rooted to the spot in shock. She could do nothing but watch in horror.

From the misshapen crater a river of thick mud flattened the forest and flowed to the beach. Tiny figures tried to launch their vessels, but there was nowhere to hide. The rain of fiery volcanic rocks showered the minute figures paddling desperately in the boats. The sea was a boiling grey monster. The land had gone mad. The volcano goddess had lost her mind.

The woman stared at the trail of mud and broken trees. Flotsam of smashed wood bobbed on the dirty waves. She scoured the scene for her people but she could see no one. Could she be the only living soul left on the island?

Disbelief gave an air of unreality to it all. Her people were gone. In a matter of minutes her beautiful green paradise had become a charred wasteland. The woman wanted desperately not to see but she couldn't tear her eyes away. In the session Dominic wasn't sure he wanted to see either, but just like the woman he couldn't help himself.

With another boom the volcano exploded again. From the depths of the mountain the crazed volcano goddess vomited a bright ball of fire across the island. It was heading straight for the woman. It was all happening terribly fast, yet the ball of fire seemed to hurtle towards the rocks in slow motion. She knew it was the end for her.

At that point Dominic suddenly interrupted the session. Sitting up, he declared he had seen enough for the moment. He wasn't in a hurry to see his own death today thank you; it could wait until next week.

Dominic took a deep breath. He looked around the room, getting his bearings in the present. Still half on the island, Dominic was torn between wanting to see and not wanting to. It was all too intense. He wanted some time to think about the whole experience before going to that island again.

Early the following morning, however, Dominic rang, saying a week was way too long and could he please have an earlier appointment. That evening he was back, eager to take advantage of the immediacy of the previous day's experience.

Dominic turned his awareness inward, entering the inner space. He felt an immense nostalgia for the small tropical island. It had always been a welcoming and joyful place, from its forests filled with lush tropical fruit, to the sea abundant with colourful fish. Even the air had a kind of brightness to it. The people were happy on their island home. It was a good life, harmoniously nestled between the fiery mountain goddess and the spirit of the ocean.

Growing up on the island was like living in one big family with many fathers and mothers. Dominic described the women as hard working and friendly and the men as handsome and good natured. There was no striving or suffering and everyone was loved.

There was a man with black hair and kind eyes who loved the woman. The pair had known each other since they first learned to walk. They had played together, dug for shellfish on the beach, and later discovered sex with each other. The woman knew her friend would always be there. Unlike the other young women, she was in no hurry to grow up and have her own family. She liked her life the way it was, all pleasure and fun with no responsibility.

Dominic was filled with nostalgia for that idyllic life. This brought him straight back to the dreadful day when he had seen paradise destroy itself. It seemed only moments since the first terrible rumble had hushed the birdsong till the beautiful island had become nothing but mud and ash. The woman's island was dying, and she was being forced to witness it. If she closed her eyes she could still feel and smell and hear it all. There was no way to save herself. Frozen with panic, she stared at a world now beyond her comprehension.

The ball of fire was flying towards the woman and she knew she was living her last moments. Many things flashed through her mind. Her man was away fishing. Would he return to this blackened hell or was he already dead? She regretted not having given him more of herself. She could have made him so happy had she married him and given him a child. She had been too interested in pleasure and good times and now everything was ending.

Ahead of the fireball came a deadly hot wind. There was a slight shock as the wall of heat hit her, and then . . . nothing. Although she felt just as if she was still standing there on the rocks, when she looked at her body it was burnt black like all the trees and grasses around. She was made of charcoal, hardened and brittle like a statue. Confused, the woman didn't know what to do. She thought she would stay there until the world turned green again and the nightmare was over. Her beautiful life would return.

Then the woman realised her charred body had fallen to the ground and she was floating above it. Seeing her body dead was even more bewildering. She could think of only one thing: keep still and wait for everything to go back to normal. She was disoriented and distressed. All she wanted was to have her island back the way it was. She was too young to die. She had been cheated out of her perfect life. In the inner space, Dominic was feeling the woman's loss as his own.

When Dominic was asked to see what happened next, a symbolic vision opened up for him. Whether it was minutes or aeons later he couldn't say, but he still felt very much like the island woman.

Dominic was in a dreamy scene, lying on his belly among puffy white clouds, looking down at Earth. Through each hole in the clouds was a possible next life for the island woman. Seeing an island and a volcano, she leaped into it without hesitation, desperate to be home again. Just as Dominic's past self jumped she saw it was the wrong island. She landed on a Mediterranean island where life was more formal, with clothes and schools and work. This was a life chosen for the wrong reasons. It would not make her happy, but it was already too late to go back.

To Dominic it seemed that barely a moment had passed before his past self had incarnated again. The island woman had yearned so intensely for her home that she completely missed the after-life journey into subtle spiritual realms. Whether his between-life experience had really happened like this, Dominic couldn't tell. Jumping through clouds wasn't exactly the way he had envisaged the incarnation process. It was, however, a telling metaphor for the way he had chosen his next life.

When Dominic was asked if he could see any parallel between the island life and his present one he said he could. Managing his corporation didn't leave him much time for idle pleasures, however he did have a strong reaction to seeing things he didn't like. He would try to look away, just as the islander woman had. Even after she was dead she had not wanted to see it was finished and tried desperately to return to her beautiful island.

Dominic had always felt a great affinity, even nostalgia, for the Pacific islands. He had spent some time in Vanuatu, a cluster of volcanic islands in the South Pacific. He felt greatly attracted to the lifestyle, the climate and the general ambiance of the land there. He also had a fascination for volcanoes, having trekked on them in several different parts of the world.

Dominic continued with the sessions, experiencing more past lives and consistently returning to the theme of not wanting to see. The difference between the past and the present was that now Dominic did want to see. He was tired of the superficiality of his social life. Parties and people bored him. Real meaning, he knew, was to be found within himself.

Interestingly, some time later Dominic saw another life involving an erupting volcano. This time he was a man running on flat ground. This volcano was low and rounded, and he could see orange lava flowing from its sides. There was the smell of sulphur and burning trees, and a deadly rain of charcoal and hot pebbles. Gasping for breath as he ran, the man felt the hot sulphurous air in his throat and the deep rumble of the volcano through his whole body.

In this second volcano experience Dominic's past self was more angry than afraid. There was even a not quite acknowledged thought of, 'Oh no, not again'. To him it was a personal battle between man and volcano. Fighting for every burning breath, he ran to his boat and paddled for his life. After many hours in the water, the man reached the safety of a neighbouring island where he was given a hero's welcome by its inhabitants. Dominic noted that looking for others to take with him to safety hadn't even occurred to that man.

Dominic commented that although the two volcano experiences were very different, both his past selves had the same selfish preoccupation with their own interests. He pledged to himself that this life would not follow that pattern. He did not want one more realisation, at the moment of death, that he had once again wasted his life on selfish trivialities.

28
THE LEPER'S HEALING
Hannah

Hannah was a youngish grandmother in her mid forties with a busy life. By day she took care of her small grandson and two nights a week she taught an interior design course at evening college. There was no time in Hannah's life to get bored. Recently an odd rash had developed on Hannah's hands. It had begun in the centre of each palm and over the following weeks had spread to her wrists and fingers. Hannah's skin was red, itchy and flaky, and sometimes it cracked and bled. The rash was a painful nuisance.

Hannah's doctor said it was eczema and prescribed an ointment. A second opinion from a dermatologist produced a diagnosis of psoriasis, and a prescription for a different ointment. Hannah hesitated. Now that she knew the rash wasn't dangerous she wasn't ready to fill either prescription just yet. She had the feeling there was a deeper level to the appearance of this odd rash.

Already engaged in some past-life exploration, Hannah decided to seek the source of her rash in ISIS, in case it had a non-medical cause the doctors couldn't see. The rash had been there for fifteen months anyway—no doubt she would cope for a few weeks longer. At the very least, sourcing the rash offered an opportunity to learn something about herself.

As the session began Hannah saw herself as a man in a hot dry place dotted with olive trees. He wore a long robe and covered his head to protect himself from the unrelenting sun. The man's homeland was occupied by a foreign army, and was patrolled by soldiers wearing short tunics and shiny breastplates. The man's community had retreated to the desert hills to avoid the constant presence of the occupation. There they lived in cool dry caves, going out to nearby towns whenever they had to buy and trade.

Hannah had the sense the country she was seeing might be Judea—present-day Israel—in the time of the Roman occupation. She saw the man gathering firewood. It was early morning and the sun had not yet reached its full heat. His attention was drawn to a small crowd of men and women following a man who was speaking to them as they walked.

The man's audience appeared to be listening intently and asking questions. Small children jostled to walk next to him and hold his hand. As the man squinted in the bright sunlight he saw that the leader was describing the shape of a cross in the air with his hands. There was something about him that intrigued the firewood gatherer. From afar it seemed as if the speaker's hands left small trails of light in the air. There was something special going on there. The man moved closer to the crowd. He was curious. He couldn't have said why, but he felt an inexplicable pull to be near that man.

Joining the group of men and women, the man fell into step behind the teacher and was soon drinking in his words. This leader was speaking about the active nature of love. Real love, the man was telling his students, is a doing and a giving. Actively caring for someone is one of the most noble things a human being can do. The flight of angels is powered by caring.

The teacher's words were strange to the man's mind and yet they spoke to his heart. He didn't completely understand them but they made him feel inspired, as he was when watching the sun rise or holding a new baby. He became engrossed in the teaching, forgetting to add more sticks of firewood to his bundle. After a while he looked around him. It seemed as though only minutes had passed but already it was sunset.

The teacher gazed around at the faces of his students and noticed the man standing there, still carrying a bundle of firewood on his back. He came up to him and without a word, looked him in the eyes and touched his fingers lightly on the man's chest. All at once a tremendous joy flared in the man and his heart began to shine like the sun. Hunger, heat and fatigue vanished. He felt alive like never before. Immediately he knew he wanted to follow this man. Had someone asked him, he couldn't have articulated why. He just knew. That night at home he said his goodbyes and the next day he left the caves to walk with the teacher, wherever he might go.

After that the man learned to heal people through touch. He would draw on the light of his teacher's love and give it to those who asked him for help. Men and women with leprosy, poor souls whom no one would touch or come near, would approach him for healing. By touching the lepers with his hands, he gave them his healing energy. Some who were not yet riddled with the disease would be healed. Others already on their deathbed would cross over peacefully to the afterlife, carried softly by the light he gave them from his heart.

Each time the healer touched a sick person his hands would become hot. Hannah felt herself as the healer, and felt the energy radiating from his palms. A great compassion would surge through him and envelope the person he was touching. The more receptive the sick person was to his compassion, the more powerful the healing. Those who could receive the most went away changed not only in body but in spirit.

Materially it was a simple life but it was rich with spiritual depth. The healer was devoted to his teacher. Learning under this man's guidance brought him tremendous joy. Later he travelled alone but continued to feel nourished through the love he held for the teacher. He carried out his healing work in the knowledge he was serving the Divine. He felt his life had meaning and purpose.

After some years of this the healer contracted leprosy himself. It began on the palm of each hand with two sores that refused to heal, and spread slowly and relentlessly through his body. At first the healer was not worried. He was certain he too would be healed before long. After all, he was an instrument for God's work. He trusted the healing force he gave to others would also work its miracle on him. Then, as he saw his body rotting away, he grew more afraid. He had seen what it was like to die of this ugly wasting disease. He grew angry with God. He was a good person. Couldn't God see he was serving Him? Why didn't He protect him?

Hannah felt the healer's fear and outrage as he saw himself about to die a poor, despised leper. After all he had given, God was cruel to let him perish like this, eaten away by the very disease he had healed in others. He was angry at God, angry at his teacher, and angry at himself for trusting so innocently. Like this he died, distanced from the loving compassion and healing light he had spent so many years bringing to others.

In the session Hannah was angry, too. The anger was like a heat that boiled inside her and made her want to shout and scream. Angry sounds were soon pouring from Hannah's mouth as she vented her outrage of being abandoned by God. The outpouring brought a wonderful feeling of transgression. To let herself get so furious and to hear the wild primal sounds issuing from her mouth took Hannah totally away from her normal mental standpoint. Her belly was a primitive beast and she screamed for the sheer exhilarating joy of it.

In the midst of the experience Hannah was struck by the incongruity of the situation. This was not at all what she had expected past-life therapy to be. Was this any way for a responsible middle-aged woman to behave? Intoxicated by the forces awakening in her belly, Hannah started laughing. She laughed and laughed until she was completely out of breath and then finally she lay still, a smile still on her lips.

In the ensuing silence Hannah felt like a new person. She was not only light-headed but felt light-bodied as if floating on a sunbeam. Buoyed up by the feeling of light, Hannah realised the lightness was coming from her own heart. The anger had gone and she realised the feeling of light in herself was the same as she had experienced as the healer in that long-ago life in Judea. Her past self had called it God. To Hannah it held the essence of her real self.

Overcome by leprosy and anger, the healer had lost touch with this light. Now Hannah saw it had never left him. Even in that ugly, angry death, the light had been there, patiently waiting. Had the healer only turned towards it he would have found solace, despite what was happening to his body. Hannah sighed. It didn't make sense to her pragmatic side, however she understood that there are things of the heart that the mind will never understand. It was like a long-awaited reunion with someone she loved deeply. Hannah was shedding tears of joy.

That session was a momentous turning point for Hannah. In the days that followed she found herself bursting into song at odd moments. Her singing came straight from the heart. A door that had been closed was open again.

In the ensuing days and weeks Hannah was amazed to see changes in her painful rash. The broken skin healed over and became hot and intensely itchy. Then, slowly, the rash started to diminish. Incredulously Hannah watched as the angry redness gradually retreated to the middle of her palms where it had started. Eventually both hands were totally clear, as if the rash had never existed.

Several years later Hannah's skin remained perfectly smooth. The way she saw it, the rash had been her body's attempt to get rid of that old anger from lifetimes ago. Now that it had found its way out, there was no need for the rash any more.

29
WARNING FROM THE FUTURE
Christina

Christina didn't have many friends and had never considered this a problem—until she encountered her new boyfriend's wide social circle. She was irritated by their open-armed welcome. They didn't even know her yet. How could they possibly be genuine? Christina resented sharing her partner with his entourage of workmates, football club members and old school buddies. It didn't help that, although he was warm and loving when they were alone together, his work often took him away for days or weeks at a time. After a few heated discussions Christina and Harry agreed that her reactions were signalling something she needed to sort out within herself.

In her sessions Christina saw a curly-haired man wearing a military uniform. The man's jacket was covered with buttons and medals and he stood tall and proud. However, this didn't feel to Christina like a past life at all. Rather, she had the clear sense that she was seeing herself in a possible future life.

The military officer in Christina's inner vision was reliable and decisive. He had an air of quiet authority about him and Christina could see he commanded respect among his peers and subordinates.

Christina saw her future self in the midst of a strategy meeting with other officers. They were seated round a large table strewn with papers and maps and the tension was almost tangible. They were about to make a ruthless move. For the sake of gaining ground with the enemy, some of their own people would have to be sacrificed.

The man in Christina's vision had made heart-wrenching decisions before, but this time it was different. The proposed strategy would allow the enemy to take over the area where his own wife and child lived. This would draw enemy troops away from other strategic positions, making them vulnerable.

The officer maintained his countenance as he took in the full implications of what they were about to do. The operation would cause civilian casualties. He might be in the process of planning the death of his own family. Getting them out beforehand would not be possible. It would be noticed by the enemy and possibly cause panic in the town, and the operation's success would rely greatly on the element of surprise.

From a military perspective it was clear what he must do, but from a personal standpoint the officer was torn apart. He was faced with a choice between the ideal of human rights that he had always fought for and the family he loved. There was nowhere for him to turn.

After the meeting the officer tried to call his wife. He could reach only her message service. Unable to rest he paced in the small cabin, going over and over the situation in his mind, desperate to find an alternative.

His wife was his joy and his strength, the one person he could turn to for support when everyone else was looking to him for leadership. His heart broke to think of losing her. And their son—the last time he had seen him was six months ago, for the boy's fourth birthday. It devastated him to think his child's life might end soon, and by his own hand. His normally unshakeable composure lost, the officer felt he was in freefall.

Over and over he ran through the plan. He couldn't believe what his superior officers expected him to do. He could hardly breathe for the tightness in his chest. As his pain turned to anger, the man cursed his commanding officers, then the warmongering enemy leaders, and then the forces of divinity themselves. He wanted to fight for freedom, but at what cost? He was not ready to risk losing the two people he loved most.

Anger took over the officer's heart and cut him off from the principles of integrity he lived by. In his rage the officer kicked at the cabin walls and swore. It wasn't right. They were asking too much of him. He was in more emotional pain than he had ever felt and getting angry was only making it worse. He lost all clarity and objectivity. Clenching his fists, he decided he would not let his family be sacrificed for the sake of winning a battle. He would not desert his loved ones for principles. To hell with principles—from now on he would fight according to his own rules.

A wave of black hatred rose up inside him. He was vengeful and dangerous, in opposition to the every ideal he had stood for. His only option, he decided, would be to sabotage the entire operation.

Christina was alarmed at the way she saw her future self making this decision. Something was going very wrong. This man was supposed to be a key player for the light. If he deserted his own sense of integrity then by default he would be serving not only the enemy but the forces of darkness.

Christina searched deep inside herself for the meaning of what she was seeing. Her future self was carrying something unresolved from his past—a shard of dark anger that was making him lose his discernment at this crucial time. Christina understood that this was a warning. She must address her buried anger or there was every chance she would end up like the future man.

Such vision brings power. Seeing the possible direction her future self would choose was an invitation to change it. Christina's vision was telling her to resolve her anger before it got the better of her.

Christina's next sessions were firmly focused on this life. Since seeing her future self she had done some honest thinking about her anger and had to admit it was an issue. Like that future man, she found it easier to shout angrily and kick things than to cry when things went wrong. Christina had always hated being told what to do, and as a child she had thrown tantrums regularly. Even now she was known among her friends for having a temper.

Christina explored her childhood and she saw the lack of caring she had grown up with. Busy parents and older siblings had meant Christina was often left on her own. As a small girl, throwing a tantrum was frequently the only way she could guarantee getting some parental attention. Even being scolded was better than being ignored.

Over the time Christina came to the sessions it became clear she was much happier when her partner Harry was at home and her sensual side had plenty of scope for expression. On the other hand, when Harry was working out of town Christina would become grumpy and irritable.

Christina agreed with this observation. She tended to feel happier, stronger and more centred when she received plenty of loving. She had an enormous potential for sensuality and pleasure and she had seldom found partners who matched her. Too often in the past Christina had been with men who had no idea what to do with her intensity. She had learned to hold herself back for fear of scaring her partners away. This had been at her own expense. A huge amount of frustration had built up inside and was expressing itself in all sorts of unrelated situations.

Christina had never thought too much about the link

between anger and sexuality. She had strong sexual yearnings but had always covered them up, afraid of where they might lead her. Hadn't she always been taught that nice girls shouldn't be too sexual? There was no place for intense libido in her belief system. She had tried to concentrate on being a 'nice' girlfriend and partner. The trouble was, feeling unmatched in most of her relationships had not done much for her niceness.

It was suggested to Christina that there may not be anything nice about repressing such a gloriously passionate aspect of herself and she was invited to take a different attitude. Why not embrace her sensuality as part of knowing and being her real self? Through working on this within her relationship, and in the internalised space of ISIS, she had the perfect opportunity to explore and own the subtle life energies that were her sensuality and sexuality.

Christina was guided through the hidden levels of consciousness in her belly. The space deepened and soon she felt like she was diving through a deep luminous pool.

In her inner vision Christina perceived herself in an emerald cavern. It was rich with the power of creativity. The air glowed with greenish light and the sides of the cave were studded with strange gems. Juicy fruit-like emeralds, strong with the forces of life, glowed from the cavern's walls. Simply by looking at them Christina was inundated with their vibrant healing waves.

At first she was tentative. What sort of place was this? Was it real or imaginary? Whatever it was, being there made her feel fantastic, as if she was in the afterglow that follows great lovemaking, or the ocean that was once witness to the secret beginnings of life. It didn't make sense to Christina's logical mind but it spoke volumes to her more instinctive side.

After this session Christina wanted to put it all together. What did that fabulous green cavern have to do with the future, or with her now? It all made sense somewhere but Christina needed to think it through.

Seldom in her life had Christina really got what she wanted. Her childhood had been starved of emotional nurturing and now she was in a relationship with a loving but often absent partner. She was frequently on her own and had become accustomed to feeling unmatched and unsatisfied sexually. Her negative attitude had become a self-fulfilling prophecy. She expected disappointment and gave up trying too easily. Although she was outwardly cheerful, inside she was a seething pool of disappointment.

Christina could see that if she were to continue like this the resentment would build up inside her like steam in a pressure-cooker. This unresolved anger would burst out eventually and annihilate any chance of clear judgment, probably just when she most needed to keep her cool. Her vision of the future had made this clear.

Over the next few months Christina focused on her relationship and worked sincerely on learning intimacy and trust. As her sessions uncovered layers of anger and hurt, her cynical attitude towards Harry's friends started to soften. She was also discovering new levels of warmth and trust with Harry.

Christina looked at where her inner journey had taken her. She had started with the discomfort she felt with her partner's welcoming friends but had found this was just the tip of the iceberg. She had seen her own possible future as well as the deep magical cavern of her sensuality. She understood herself on a deeper level and was creating positive changes in her life. Christina knew very well how much her attitudes, habits and choices were shaping her future.

30
LIVING IN THE PRESENT

Break the moulds of the past,
but keep safe its gains and its spirit,
or else you have no future.
Sri Aurobindo

Despite the retrospection its name implies, past-life therapy is firmly grounded in the present. The work of sourcing begins with present-day issues, and guides people through the past to bring in tangible results in the here-and-now.

Jade, who was once unable to sustain a harmonious relationship with fellow workers, found a rewarding job, renewed health and vitality and a new depth of love in her relationship. Giannetta and Eric each faced their fear of holding power and both went on to become enthusiastic and effective team leaders. Sally shed her phobias and revealed a spiritual dimension within herself that she had been missing. Hannah healed her mysterious eczema and discovered a new level of joy in life. Alex let go of his bitterness and saw a world of possibilities opening up for him.

Without a way to see through the smokescreen of their own conditioning, most people live in a distorted reality created by their samskaras. Every reaction, every emotion and every mood is conditioned by samskaras, whether they realise it or not. A baby boy clings to his mother after his parents divorce, then grows up to form dependent relationships with older women. A married woman loses confidence in her femininity after her husband leaves her for a man. Traumatic events of early childhood or previous lives may be forgotten, but when the imprints are deep the passage of time does little to diminish their influence.

Not knowing about samskaras, people may believe themselves to be inherently a certain way. They say things like, 'I'm shy,' 'I have a bad temper,' 'I detest having my photo taken,' 'It's just the way I am.' However, idiosyncrasies can hide layers of conditioning. Even seemingly trivial likes and dislikes can be samskara based. Think of Dominic, who saw how his fascination for volcanoes had originated in a past-life on a volcanic island; or Elaine, whose abhorrence of pain was a legacy from a painful love affair lifetimes ago. All sorts of limitations, big and small, can stem from samskaras, and that is the key to changing them. If the conditioning had a beginning then it can also have an end.

To many people, even to those starting therapy, the idea that their personality could change at a fundamental level is not obvious. They want to feel better, to solve their problems and be happy. But become different? Most people don't even know what that could mean.

When people go to the depths of themselves, however, they do become different and the results show in their lives. They rediscover their enthusiasm and sense of purpose. Their eyes shine. They look younger. Old limiting habits fall away and they start taking control of their lives. At times the change seen in people is striking. However, to the individuals themselves, even the most dramatic change feels perfectly normal. They know they are becoming more themselves.

When someone experiences past events at their source in the inner space, all manner of destructive and negative patterns can be brought to light and unravelled. Bit by bit, the samskaras lose their power and conditioned behaviour is replaced by emotional clarity and free will.

Besides being a catalyst for creating a better life, the work of sourcing often leads to profound spiritual openings. The dissolution of a samskara comes with illuminating flashes of self-awareness and expanded states of spiritual vision. These liberated states are not just enjoyable experiences that happen as a kind of bonus during the sessions; they lie at the very core of the ISIS process. Seen in this light, samskaras are far more than blockages; they are gateways to experiencing the higher aspects of human consciousness.

Fortunately, to lead to beautiful states of spiritual opening, past-life experiences do not have to be historically accurate, or even close to it. Whether they are factual or not is not the point. The important thing is that they are *emotionally accurate*.

Past-life therapy can open up all sorts of subtle experiences. It awakens vision. It opens the door to levels of reality that are inaccessible to the ordinary mental consciousness. At times people may find themselves inundated with brilliant non-physical light and spiritual presence in the inner space, like Christina's experience of the life-giving emerald cavern. One man felt as if his consciousness was spread through deep space and his body had turned into a shining cloud of stars.

At a logical level none of this makes sense, but there are levels where it does not have to. Such beyond-the-mind experiences put people in touch with the eternal parts of themselves, the parts that exist beyond the limitations of time. They bring a density of presence and a certitude that nothing could be more real. During such experiences, normal life appears like a two-dimensional cardboard reality.

The immense changes that deep inner work such as ISIS brings about are not vague or theoretical, but tangible and practical. Fears dissipate, health and energy levels improve, tangled emotional issues are straightened out, and relationship difficulties clarify. Past-life therapy is not a panacea of course—no therapy is one hundred percent effective for everyone. For those who apply themselves to the process, though, the results are plainly visible in their lives. It's not unusual for friends or family to notice the difference and wonder what they have been doing recently.

Interestingly, the people for whom past-life therapy brings the biggest changes are not those blessed by some special talent or vision, but individuals with an underlying desire to know themselves. Again and again it can be seen how past-life experiences bring profound personal insights about the present. It is more than an intellectual understanding. As well as bringing resolution of samskaras and knowledge of past lives, the direct experience of having existed beyond the here and now has a powerful awakening effect. After that, life just cannot look quite the same.

NOTES

Introduction

Samuel Sagan, *Aphorisms, Not All of Them Related to the Clairvision Work,* 1995.

Chapter 6

IP Pavlov, *Conditioned Reflexes*, translator GV Anrep, Dover Publications, 1984.

S Sagan, *Regression, Past-Life Therapy for Here and Now Freedom*, Section 3.2, Clairvision School Foundation, Sydney, 2006.

Chapter 21

S Aurobindo, *Pensées et Aphorismes, tome 2*, aphorism number 228, Buchet/Chastel, Paris, 1984.

S Sagan, *Aquila* lecture cycle, unpublished lectures Tuesday 20 June 1995, Clairvision Knowledge Base, Clairvision School Ltd, Sydney, 1999.

R Steiner, *Karmic Relationships*, Rudolf Steiner Press, Dornach, 1924.

Chapter 26

P Hauri, 'Evening activity, sleep mentation, and subjective sleep quality' *Journal of Abnormal Psychology*, 1970, vol 76(2) 270–275.

S Sagan, *Death, the Great Journey*, Clairvision Knowledge Track (correspondence course), Sydney, 2001.

HA Witkin, HB Lewis 'The relation of experimentally induced presleep experiences to dreams—a report on method and preliminary findings', *Journal of the American Psychoanalytic Association*, 1965, 13:819–849.

Chapter 30

S Aurobindo, *Pensées et Aphorismes, tome 2*, aphorism number 238, Buchet/Chastel, Paris, 1984.

ISIS is taught by the Clairvision® school and practised by IST practitioners worldwide. You can read more on the IST website: www.innerspacetechniques.com.

Clairvision® is a school of meditation and spiritual work that offers courses worldwide. For more, visit the Clairvision website: www.clairvision.org.